6/1

12. *Kiyokawa Family Orchards, Parkdale, OR*
13. *Paul's Grains, Laurel, IA*
14. *Red Lake Nation Foods, Red Lake, MN*
15. *Ronnybrook Farm Dairy, Ancramdale, NY*

16. *Joseph Fields Farm, John's Island, SC*
17. *Garcia Organic Farms, Fallbrook, CA*
18. *Riverview Farms, Ranger, GA*

"A beautiful, bountiful tribute to the local heroes who are sustaining America's proud farming heritage and putting fresh, organic food on our tables. Between the captivating farm profiles and the fresh-from-the-field recipes, *Growing Tomorrow* is sure to inspire future generations of farmers and home cooks everywhere."

—BRENT RIDGE and JOSH KILMER-PURCELL
from "The Fabulous Beekman Boys" and Beekman1802.com

"Forrest Pritchard is a farmer and talented writer giving voice to an important segment of our food world. With *Growing Tomorrow*, Pritchard trains his storytelling talents on his fellow farmers for what amounts to a portrait of America in all its extraordinary bounty. We're lucky to have this farmer-writer in our midst."

—MICHAEL RUHLMAN, author of
The Soul of a Chef: The Pursuit of Perfection

"*Growing Tomorrow* is the book that will inspire farmers, chefs, and consumers to do the right thing. A firsthand look at why sustainable farming matters and the people who are making a difference on a daily basis."

—SEAN BROCK, *New York Times***–bestselling author of** *Heritage* **and chef of**
McCrady's, Husk, and Minero

"Gorgeous, delectable, and fascinating, *Growing Tomorrow* provides food for the body, mind, and soul. Engaging to read, easy to cook from, delicious to eat, this is more than a cookbook; it is a meditation on the things that give us life."

—GARTH STEIN, *New York Times***–bestselling author of**
The Art of Racing in the Rain **and** *A Sudden Light*

"The next best thing to visiting each of the intriguing farms.
Did I hear someone say 'road trip'?"

—MARIAN BURROS, former reporter for *The New York Times* **and cookbook author**

THE EXPERIMENT
BECAUSE EVERY BOOK IS A TEST OF NEW IDEAS

"Like a flitting honey bee, master farmer/storyteller Forrest Pritchard dips our imagination into the sweet nectar of integrity farmers, pollinating our minds with petals of wisdom and practical application."
—JOEL SALATIN, owner of Polyface Farm (featured in Michael Pollan's *The Omnivore's Dilemma* and the documentary *Food, Inc.*), and author of *You Can Farm*

"Who says that nobody is going into farming these days or that you can't make a living growing foods organically and sustainably? Certainly not the 18 pioneers described in this lovely, inspiring book. Forrest Pritchard chose farmers of diverse crops—mushrooms, honey, lobsters, avocados, grain, beef, and more—and tells the personal stories of how they created lives of deep productivity and satisfaction. Any aspiring farmer or consumer of freshly farmed products will get great pleasure from reading this book and admiring its photos."
—MARION NESTLE, Professor of Nutrition, Food Studies, and Public Health at New York University, and author of *What to Eat*

"The faces of the sustainable farming movement in the US are as diverse as the crops they're growing. Forrest Pritchard has done an incredible job of telling the stories of the people who are changing the food system, one farm at a time, across the country. And with recipes from each of the farms he visits, Pritchard reminds readers how delicious food grown by people who care about the Earth can be. Pritchard is following in the steps of Wendell Berry, intertwining farming and philosophy to provide a roadmap for where the food movement is headed."
—DANIELLE NIERENBERG, President of Food Tank

"From goat cheese to wild rice, *Growing Tomorrow* will show you how today's farmers are producing healthy, delicious food using old-fashioned methods and modern technologies—truly the food we will be eating tomorrow. We get all this in Forrest Pritchard's wonderful writing style and Molly Peterson's beautiful photographs. And the recipes are yummy!"
—SALLY FALLON MORELL, President of The Weston A. Price Foundation and author of *Nourishing Traditions*

"Forrest has come into full bloom. The stories he shares in *Growing Tomorrow* create a generous and honest exhibit on the enterprise of food and the human spirit. His eloquent prose echoes both Stegner and Steinbeck in its ability to coax from the land an understanding of our relationship with it."
—BARTON SEAVER, chef and author of *For Cod and Country*

GROWING TOMORROW

A Farm-to-Table Journey
in Photos and Recipes

Behind the Scenes with
18 Extraordinary Sustainable Farmers
Who Are Changing the Way We Eat

FORREST PRITCHARD

Photographs by Molly M. Peterson

Foreword by Deborah Madison

THE EXPERIMENT

NEW YORK

Growing Tomorrow: *A Farm-to-Table Journey in Photos and Recipes*

The Experiment, LLC
220 East 23rd Street, Suite 301
New York, NY 10010-4674
www.theexperimentpublishing.com

The Experiment's books are available at special discounts when purchased in bulk for premiums
and sales promotions as well as for fund-raising or educational use. For details, contact us at info@
theexperimentpublishing.com.

Library of Congress Cataloging-in-Publication Data

Pritchard, Forrest.
  Growing tomorrow : a farm-to-table journey in photos and recipes : behind the scenes with 18
extraordinary sustainable farmers who are changing the way we eat / Forrest Pritchard ; photography by
Molly Peterson.
     pages cm
  Includes bibliographical references and index.
  ISBN 978-1-61519-284-7 (cloth) -- ISBN 978-1-61519-285-4 (ebook)
1. Sustainable agriculture--United States. 2. Local foods--United States. 3. Family farms--United States.
4. Farm produce--United States. 5. Cooking, American. I. Peterson, Molly (Molly M.) II. Title.
  S494.5.S86P755 2015
  338.10973--dc23
                          2015003785

ISBN 978-1-61519-284-7
Ebook ISBN 978-1-61519-285-4

Cover design by Christopher King
Cover photographs by Molly M. Peterson
Map illustration for endpapers by Daniel Christensen
Photograph of Forrest Pritchard by Craig McCord / Handpicked Nation
Photograph of Molly M. Peterson by Mike Peterson
Text design by Sarah Smith

Manufactured in China
Distributed by Workman Publishing Company, Inc.
Distributed simultaneously in Canada by Thomas Allen & Son Ltd.

First printing October 2015

10 9 8 7 6 5 4 3 2 1

To my fellow farmers—people of faith, creativity, and deep good humor. It's long overdue, but on behalf of our country, thanks for lunch.

The hills resound with our glad song,

And echo back to Thee;

Our thanks received for work and health,

And love and loyalty.

—"As the Bright Flames," a traditional 4-H campfire song

CONTENTS

FOREWORD

by Deborah Madison

////////////////////////////////////

Many years ago, my third-grade class took a field trip to a Hostess Cupcake factory in Sacramento. We crowded around a railing—mouths agape and eyes fixed on the steady passage of chocolate cupcakes wobbling beneath the machine that gave them their famous white squiggles. After this trip, I became fiercely loyal to these cupcakes, even though we never had them or any of their sibling pastries in our house. But because I had gotten a glimpse of the process, I had been imbued with a kind of ownership of Hostess Cupcakes. Later, I felt the same way about Veuve Clicquot Champagne after hearing the inspiring story of the widow Clicquot (veuve means widow in French). Once I knew the story (in 1805, Madame Clicquot became the first woman to head a Champagne house), the bubbles in the bottle with the orange label were mine forever, even though there were other French Champagnes I like better.

Clearly, stories make a difference.

Today third graders are more likely to take a field trip to a farm or farmers' market, and I'm confident that once they meet the farmers and taste the foods they grow, they, too, will take ownership of that experience and become faithful supporters of small-scale, sustainable agriculture, no matter where they live. *Growing Tomorrow* is a bit like a field trip—it gives readers the kind of knowledge that has the power to inspire loyalty and change, which is why it's an important book—as well as being a very good read. Forrest Pritchard introduces us to eighteen producers of the best, most delicious, and truly wholesome foods we eat. Then, he shows us their farms (or fish, flocks, or mushrooms), lets them describe their work, and tell us about their dreams, visions, and challenges with well-chosen words, pictures that sparkle and inspire, and recipes! It's so important—and so interesting—to meet the people who grow the very best food in our country.

Even if you're a faithful farmers' market shopper, it's not easy to grasp all that the farming life requires to produce good food: the hassles, the decisions that have to be made, the dependence on that changeable rascal known as weather, and the accumulated wisdom of generations. *Growing Tomorrow* is a worthwhile book in every way, including its farm source guide, which you'll definitely want to consult to help plan your own farm visits. It's hard not to build affection and admiration for every person profiled in this book—not to mention the many, many others who live lives based on the passion and hard work involved in producing food.

If you grew up on a farm, chances are it's in your blood. This book begins with the author's happy reminiscence of growing up on his grandparents' farm, which reminded me in turn of my own farm upbringing and those aspects of farm life that are so easy for a child to love. Although my experience wasn't nearly as sustained as Forrest's, the farm left a lasting impression on me and definitely got under my skin, despite my living a largely urban life. To some degree, I'm always trying to get back to the farm. Forrest actually *did* go back to his grandparents' farm and learned from the ground up what it took and how hard it was. But to many urban and suburban children, the farm is a mystery, as much a mystery as the Hostess Cupcake factory was to my classmates and me. For many Americans, food still comes from somewhere else—usually someplace far away. We don't see our food's origins; we don't see the farms or other places of production or the work, risk, and, no doubt, anxiety that goes into producing food. We don't know the histories and stories that surround food and those responsible for it; it just shows up. And we're not talking only about vegetables, but also about fruit, grain, wild rice, mushrooms, pork, beef, shellfish, cheese, and nuts—food in all, or at least many of its manifestations. *Growing Tomorrow* could well be just the ticket to open the eyes of those who still believe that milk comes from the store, not an animal, nut, or grain.

Some producers are indeed far from the urban areas they serve—a 400-acre vegetable farm *Growing Tomorrow* takes us to is one and a half hours from Chicago and a mushroom farm is three hours southwest of St. Louis. Matt Romero, a farmer from my area in northern New Mexico, is about an hour's drive from our market, which means if the market opens at seven, Matt is getting up early enough to arrive at six to set up. That's typical. But other farms are not somewhere else—they can be in cities, like D-Town Farm in Detroit where vegetables grow under the flight path of airplanes; bordered by a freeway and a suburban housing development like a vegetable farm near Washington, DC; or located in a prison, where you'll find a Colorado goat farm. Forrest Pritchard makes it happily clear that farming is not a one-size-fits-all sort of business. His book also suggests that new, young farmers are needed as most of the farmers profiled in *Growing Tomorrow* are at least in their fifties if not older, although Ras from D-Town Farm (featured on the cover) represents a new generation passionate about farming.

Chefs used to be nobodies. No one thought about being a chef—you'd go to trade school for that, and that's hardly glamorous. But starting in the 1970s, chefs began to get their day and a long day it's been. Cooking and having your own restaurant, like farming, is another career choice that's based on passion and vision, and it's also very hard work. The more we've learned about chefs, though, the more young people are inspired to follow that path. And it's now the farmers' turn to become known—for their work to be visible and acknowledged, as it is in *Growing Tomorrow*—so that we consumers know about what it takes to grow our food and get more into our bellies. As we become more appreciative, more understanding, and even inspired, perhaps some who read this book will want to become farmers, ranchers, cheese makers, or fishers. Farming will never be glamorous, but up close, most chefs' lives are not glamorous either (even as a few stand in the limelight and make it look that way). With farming, as with being a chef, the work is hard, the days are long, and your feet hurt, but farmers are absolutely happy to be in this line of work. Producing food for others is work that matters.

—DEBORAH MADISON

INTRODUCTION

G rowing up on my grandparents' farm in the late 1970s, I was afforded a diverse, panoramic view of American agriculture. Sheep and cattle grazed our West Virginia pastures, while apple and cherry orchards dotted the rolling limestone hillsides. Contoured cornfields abutted acres of wheat, yielding to purple-hued alfalfa horizons. A clutch of laying hens was always pecking in the barnyard, guarded by our fat black Labrador asleep on the porch, and each spring my grandparents planted an expansive kitchen garden. By July the rows were festooned with tomatoes, sweet corn, and pole beans. Along the edge, white beehives stood at stark angles, contrasting with the Blue Ridge Mountains forever supine in the distance.

As a young boy, I fell in love with the clovered hills, the towering hickories, the cool, silver water trickling through crisp watercress. Who wouldn't? I spent summers with my pant legs rolled, chasing minnows through the shallows of the brook, and winters jumping from barn beams into colossal heaps of harvested corn. I swashbuckled through cobwebbed barn stalls and wiggled my way out of fence-painting chores. Born a hundred years earlier, I might have found myself pen pals with Huckleberry Finn.

In 1979, my grandfather was seventy-eight and I was five. For 150 years, our family had made its living by selling fruit, grain, and livestock on the open commodity market. Now, over the course of the seventies, inflation had soared to record heights while agricultural prices dipped to catastrophic lows. Discouraged by meager wages and high operating costs, my parents—along with a generation of their peers—opted out of farming, choosing suit-and-tie jobs in the city instead. When my grandfather passed away in 1983, there was no one to replace his role as full-time farmer, and our farm fell into debt almost overnight. Within a few years the land was carved into pieces, with many large tracts sold to housing developers.

I had no way of knowing it at the time, as I watched the farm physically breaking apart, but I eventually learned that ours was an all too common story, an American tragedy unfolding in real time. US Department of Agriculture (USDA) records show that, in 1982, the average farm grossed only $9,000 while accruing more than $30,000 in debt. As it turns out, the devastation of losing our heritage was an experience shared by tens of thousands of farming families throughout the end of the century.

So it came as no surprise when, after I returned home from college in the mid-nineties, the few remaining farmers in our region strongly discouraged me from a career in agriculture. There was no money to be made, they told me. No future. I'd be trading my education for a life of hard work, endless risk, and little pay. Defeat was written on their faces. These were the same sentiments I had witnessed within my own family.

Despite the chorus of discouraging voices, it was the hope and promise of sustainable farming that spoke to me most clearly. I believed that our depleted soils were capable of producing so much more, that they could be restored, even regenerated, and coaxed once again into abundance. Like my grandfather had done more than a half-century before, I had to at least try, staking my faith that the land could provide for yet another generation. So in the summer of 1996, I shelved my résumé, laced up my work boots, and set out to rebuild our family's farm.

I quickly learned that those older farmers had been correct: It *was* hard, fraught with daily risks and unpredictable challenges. The chores were physically exhausting, and working around machinery and large livestock was often dangerous. As for money? Ha. I didn't earn a legitimate paycheck for nearly five years.

But together with my family, we slowly reinvented what was left of my grandparents' old farm. Gradually, over the course of a decade, we cultivated a successful path, finding resiliency in sustainable agriculture and our loyal, appreciative customers at nearby farmers' markets. Looking back on those difficult years, it turned out to be an incredible adventure. I chronicled this journey in my book *Gaining Ground: A Story of Farmers' Markets, Local Food, and Saving the Family Farm*, published in 2013.

As I was writing our story, I had no illusion that it was anything more than a message in a bottle, a country-mouse letter sent out into a city-mouse world. After all, with a landscape now dominated by fast-food restaurants, shopping malls, and subdivision streets ironically named for the trees bulldozed beneath their pavement, how could one farming story hope to make an impact? Publication day arrived, and my note drifted quietly out to sea.

I was stunned by the reaction: The first printing sold out in ten days. A rushed second printing sold out a few weeks later. In the months that followed, letters and reviews poured in. The responses were passionate, heartfelt, and incredibly encouraging. Many readers came from farm families themselves and had been forced to relinquish their land during the agricultural crisis of the 1980s. But even people who had never set foot on a farm wrote in with notes of hope and optimism. Collectively, they seemed to recognize a unifying idea—that nutritious food from sustainable farms benefits everyone involved, farmers and consumers alike. The concept evidently made too much sense to ignore.

The letters revealed something else, as well. Readers weren't just cheering for any one farm, or any one farmer. Instead, they wanted to see the movement *itself* succeed, creating productive, healthy farms in every community, a wholesome wave of nourishing food stretching from coast to coast. For a generation that had endured an endless stream of processed, packaged foods, weight-loss gimmicks, and celebrity fad diets, enough was finally enough. Reflecting on these letters, it struck me that people seemed to have grown tired of being jaded—at its core, cynicism is terribly draining. Sustainable farming, they insisted, was one of the few things still worth cheering for.

And that's precisely how this book came about. One evening, over dinner with friends at Waterpenny Farm, I posed the question: If one small farm could inspire such a response, what might happen if we multiplied that number? Different faces, different stories, together uniting to explain the trajectory of sustainable agriculture in America.

Immediately, I could sense excitement building around the table. Real faces, growing food with a clear and personal provenance. For my farming friends, people who had made their living this way for decades, the idea resonated instantly. *Yes.* It would be like a farmers' market dream team, someone suggested, a Saturday morning stroll through the finest market on the planet.

Brainstorming, we carried the idea a step further. The farmers could contribute their favorite recipes, sharing the best ways to cook the produce they work so hard to grow. After all, aren't farmers the original food experts? And like the farms themselves, the recipes should show variety, from the very simple to the more intricate and challenging. It would be like having a farmer in your own kitchen, explaining how the food is grown, and helping plan tomorrow's meals.

Pictures, too; we'd need lots of pictures to help tell the farms' stories. I quickly called the finest photographer around, Molly Peterson, who was every bit as enthusiastic about the project as I was. Over the next few months, we hashed out a convoluted Venn diagram of the United States, researching different farms, histories, crops, flavors, and provenances.

Sustainability in all its myriad forms—environmental, economic, generational—became our common thread, with a focus on farmers who sell directly to the public. We especially sought out different sizes and scales, from small acreages to vast expanses, to demonstrate the wide-ranging possibilities of this type of agriculture. Over the course of a year we visited eighteen different farms (check that: sixteen farms, two bee wranglers, and one fishing vessel). Traveling the country and spending time with these amazing producers was undoubtedly the journey of a lifetime. Now, it's my hope that you'll find them every bit as inspiring, generous, and hospitable as they were to us, and enjoy their unique stories as you thumb through these pages.

But please, don't stop there. If these producers inspire you, then run with it! Discover your local farms through weekend markets, Community Supported Agriculture (CSA) subscriptions, or visiting the farms themselves. Go a step further and try growing your own vegetables or tending a plot in a community garden. As Joel Salatin wisely points out in the foreword of *Gaining Ground*, not everyone was born with a green thumb or has the knack for farming. Yet as a community we can all participate, investing our food dollars into a hopeful, sustainable future.

So join me on a tour of America's sustainable farms, and grab a glimpse into the lives of the extraordinary people who grow our food. As you're reading, listen for the music—familiar harmonies for sure, cacophonies of quacks and clucks, and oinking to the beat of the band. But beyond the nursery school sounds, I hope you'll hear other music, too—the staccato rhythm of nails hammered through oak boards, or the cascading shirr of barley augured into grain bins. An old tractor wheezing and sputtering before firing once more to life, and the crooked crunch of tin snips against steel. Listen for the easy laughter of the farmers themselves, and arpeggios from songbirds filling the trees. Where words fall short, perhaps these lovely sounds will suffice.

My only regret? That I couldn't include more farmers. From Maine to Montana, Alaska to Florida, rest assured that you weren't forgotten. Rather, one book can hold only so many pages. So please, if you believe in the spirit of this project, share your feedback with my publisher (The Experiment) on Facebook and Twitter. Tell them about all the incredible farms that I missed, and the other amazing producers who deserve to be celebrated. How about cranberries? Or maple syrup? Or free-range eggs? The options, I hope you'll agree, are boundless.

I'm smiling as I type this. I've barely sat down from traveling, and I can hardly wait to do it all again.

—**FORREST PRITCHARD**
Smith Meadows Farm
March 2015

1

POTOMAC VEGETABLE FARMS

WASHINGTON, DC

Ecoganic vegetables and herbs

I t's eight thirty in the morning, and Route 7 is awash with commuters. Four lanes of traffic idle at a stoplight, awaiting the green light toward Washington, DC. As I stand in the parking lot of Potomac Vegetable Farms, the river of vehicles is no more than fifty feet away. Drivers are texting, scrolling through playlists, applying makeup. From time to time a face glances my way, studying the modest wooden vegetable stand just a few paces behind me. A moment later the light changes, and the median fills with exhaust. In the crush of the commute, with another long day on the horizon, how could anyone justify thoughts of heirloom vegetables?

Behind me, however, seventy-nine-year-old Hiu Newcomb is sorting freshly picked red, yellow, and orange tomatoes.

"These all have different names," she says without looking up, "but we don't organize them like that. We just ask folks what they're going to use them for, then point them toward the right tomato. A name can't tell you much, you know? But a farmer can."

Wizened hands float across the table, organizing, examining, occasionally discarding. A checkerboard pattern emerges before my eyes, supple yellows and rosy pinks, with a row of purple-green beauties scattered throughout for contrast.

"Here," she says, offering me a tomato the precise color of this morning's sunshine. "Taste this."

The plump orb fits neatly into my palm, and I take a bite without hesitating. The flavor is tangy and bright, with earthy notes of chicory and tarragon. No salt is required. I finish it in five satisfying bites, juice running down my fingers.

"What's this variety called?" I ask.

She shrugs. "Can't remember. But we've been growing it for forty years. Pretty good, huh?"

It's hard to imagine now, but when farmer Hiu first set foot on this property in 1959, she was going to be an elementary school music teacher. "I grew up in Honolulu, and studied piano at Oberlin, in Ohio. That's where I met this crazy farmer," she recalls with a laugh. "Our first day of freshman orientation. Tony was a dreamer. A dreamer with big farming plans."

Tony wanted to return east and create an agricultural community he grandly named "Kingdom on the James," a reference to the nearby James River. But before breaking ground on this new project, the newlyweds decided they should actually learn a little something about farming. "As a teenager," Hiu recalls, "Tony inherited a tractor. He figured that if you had a tractor and a plow and some seeds, then the farm would pretty much take care of itself. Boy, did we have a lot to learn."

Now, Hiu's farm is a fifteen-acre oasis in the center of Mid-Atlantic suburbia. It's late August, and the summer has been especially kind: Cool temperatures and plentiful rains kept watering to a minimum. Verdant rows of green beans, zinnias, tomatillos, and blackberries contour the gently rolling Piedmont hills. As Hiu passes near her eastern property line, however, she frowns.

Did You Know?

In *Nix v. Hedden*, 1893, the Supreme Court unanimously ruled that the tomato is a vegetable, not a fruit, thereby settling an import tax dispute.

"This is a field we recently repurchased after many years. It served as an access road to the subdivision next door, and over the years it's been bulldozed, paved over, you name it. Rather pathetic to look at, but we're doing our best to bring it back to life." She winks. "We've got a running joke: 'This is the only place where asphalt was lost to farmland, and not the other way around.'"

Compared to the splendor of the rest of the farm, I can't deny that this half acre looks particularly anemic. Triangular in shape, it points like an arrowhead toward the neighboring suburbs, the houses sitting no more than twenty feet away from the other side of the fence. "We've been adding compost, sowing cover crops. But you can see from the plants how weak this soil is, how different it is from the rest of the farm."

Suddenly, she brightens. "We'll eventually bring it back to life, though. Everything just takes a little time."

It's precisely this sort of optimism—a faith in nature's resilience and the healing power of time—that's helped Potomac Vegetable Farms navigate decades of rocky terrain. These days, Hiu can occasionally take a risk or two, investing time into a piece of ground that might take an entire generation to rebuild. But it wasn't always like this.

"When Tony and I started out, we could only afford to rent land year-to-year. We'd sign a lease on ten acres here, thirty acres there, and plant sweet corn. This was the early 1960s, and even back then development was going full tilt—no one was seriously thinking about farming for a living. We'd rent the fields for fifteen dollars an acre, and farm it until the developers showed up. Most of the ground we leased back then is a subdivision now, or a strip mall."

After several seasons of farming, they finally decided to buy. Against the advice of fellow farmers and university agriculture specialists, the young couple bought a parcel of land on the sandy soils of southern Maryland, a narrow tract comprising 140 acres. It was rough going from the start. An old farmhouse on the property had been abandoned for decades, and there was no electricity or piped water. Before they knew it, they had two young children to look after, with a third on the way.

"Looking back, I'm not sure how we did it. Beyond the Maryland farm, we were still renting acreage here in northern Virginia, going back and forth several hours each week. Farming here and there, all the while trying to raise a family. Start a homestead. Pay the bills.

"But we were learning," she adds thoughtfully. "Learning what type of vegetables we could grow, and how to market them. We gradually began to plant less sweet corn, and focused on diversifying: melons, beans, tomatoes. Squash and zucchini. A little less wholesale each year, a little more retail instead. More balance in the system."

Hiu's dreams of becoming a music teacher gradually faded. Now with a fourth child, crops to plant, and a business to run, she fully embraced the life of the family farm.

"I was in the fields twelve hours a day and cooking dinner each night before putting the kids to bed. Then, one night while we were working up here in Virginia, we get a call: Our house in Maryland was on fire. An arsonist had broken in while we were away. By the time the firefighters got there, only the brick chimneys were left."

Standing in the rubble of the family homestead might be enough to break

Hiu's Farming Wisdom

"Rent land before buying it. Cash inflow must exceed outflow, and that's hard to do with a mortgage."

most people's resolve. But Hiu and Tony took it as a sign. "We were trying to do too much, stretched too thin. In a way it was a blessing, because that's when we decided to buy this piece of land near Tysons Corner and really got things going."

Like any practical farmer, they managed to salvage some of the wreckage. They transported the scorched bricks of their Maryland farm to the property in Virginia, newly dubbed Potomac Vegetable Farms, and laid a masonry pathway. "Historically, the bricks had been used as ballast in ships coming over from England in the 1700s," Hiu explains. "It only seemed proper that we repurpose them one more time."

The years passed, and the new farm flourished. They opened a vegetable stand beside the highway that ran along their property, catering to Washington commuters. Four young children grew into teenagers throughout the 1970s, and the farm provided all the food their family needed. "We didn't know what 'fast food' was," she recalls sincerely, "and the thought of buying processed food—you know, food that comes from a box—it just never even occurred to us. We had corn, lettuce, beans. Eggplants and sweet potatoes. The land gave us all the food we needed."

Tony and Hiu began to hire recent college graduates, teaching them how to farm and imparting economic lessons not taught in school. Then, in 1980, they were among the first farms to sign up for a new agricultural experiment, thoroughly untested and utterly unproven in the DC region. They would be attending something called a "farmers' market."

"You have to understand," Hiu elaborates. "These days, nearly every small town has a farmers' market. But back in the seventies and eighties, hardly anyone had even heard of such a thing. Yet there we were, showing up on the first day with green beans and tomatoes, not

knowing what to expect . . . and the people were so excited to see us! It was almost as though they had been waiting for us this whole time. Our vegetables practically flew off the table."

Farmers' markets quickly defined the next era of success for PVF, and as more markets popped up, they became early adopters of this new opportunity. But while the markets were an immediate success, Hiu and Tony's personal life had reached a crossroads. Decades of farming and financial stress had taken their toll, and in 1982 the couple agreed to an amicable separation.

Tony returned to Maryland to rebuild the old homestead and begin farming anew. All the while, he had never forgotten his dreams of creating a sustainable agricultural community, and in the evenings he sketched a plan that would later take shape as Blueberry Hill, a fifteen-house community built around the farm in Virginia. Then, tragedy struck a second time.

"All of a sudden, he couldn't keep his breath," Hiu recalls. "Back when we first started out, we'd use chemicals on the sweet corn, pesticides and sprays. We never even thought about using a respirator or protective clothing; we'd just spread the chemicals around by hand. I'm convinced that's what caused Tony's cancer. By the time he visited the doctor, there was really nothing that could be done."

In 1984, Tony's children buried their father on the Virginia farm, near where he planned to break ground for his farming community. More than thirty years later, Blueberry Hill is a resounding success, fully occupied with a robust waiting list.

Hiu pauses at a bed of parsley. "Now that I think of it, I need to pick seventy-five bunches for our CSA members this afternoon. Would you mind helping me harvest?"

What's a CSA?

An acronym for Community Supported Agriculture, CSA members pay their farmer a fixed price at the beginning of the year, then receive a weekly or bi-weekly share of fresh produce or other goods for the duration of the season. This provides farmers with much-needed starting revenue, and guarantees fresh, local food for the customers. Since the early eighties, CSAs nationwide have blossomed from a few dozen to more than thirteen thousand.

It's a cloudless morning, and the sun warms our backs as we lean over the beds. I chew absently on a sprig of parsley as we work, and the flavor is peppery yet mild, the aroma reminiscent of freshly cured alfalfa hay. We gather the herbs into fist-size bundles, wrapping a rubber band around the stems. As I stand to stretch, I can't help but notice the row of enormous houses abutting the farm, brick fronts with vinyl-sided backs, their immaculately landscaped lawns ending just at the edge of the vegetable field.

"This is our 'new normal,'" Hiu says. "All of these houses were built in the last five years or so, and our farm is now split in two. After development started, we petitioned for a special right-of-way from the homeowners association so we can drive our carts from one side of our farm to the other."

I ask her how many of her new neighbors shop at the farm stand. "Oh, probably not many. But it's hard to say." She pauses. "Part of me believes the next generation of customers is starting to see the value in what we do. Of course, if they do choose to shop with us, it probably doesn't hurt that we're right in their own backyard."

The next generation always seems to be on Hiu's mind. As we load the parsley onto her golf cart, she reveals a small secret. "My daughter Hana doesn't let me drive the tractor anymore." A wistful note lingers in her voice, but it quickly disappears. "This is her farm now, really, and rightfully so. It's the natural course of things. She's proven herself to be an excellent manager, and at this stage of my career, I'm perfectly happy doing what she tells me."

An even younger generation is now helping on the farm. As we ride back to the vegetable stand, Hiu's grandsons Steven and Michael flash past on a cart of their own, waving as gravel skitters in their wake.

"And will your grandchildren take over the farm after Hana?" I ask.

"Hard to say," she replies, guiding our cart through the housing development. "But we've always got a backup plan. Hana's motto is 'Hire talent.' We've hired our fair share of great folks over the years, and we know that the farm will be in good hands no matter what happens."

We arrive back at the packing shed, where rows of CSA bags are being stocked for the weekly distribution. The parsley, evidently, has arrived just in time. "Sorry to cut the interview short," she says, smiling, "but I've got to load the van and make a delivery. Hungry people waiting. I'm sure you can understand."

Hiu's Farming Wisdom

Ever heard the expression "barefoot hippies"? Working barefoot actually can be practical: "If you step on a tomato vine wearing shoes," Hiu explains, "the vine is crushed . . . and when you grow thousands of tomatoes, it's hard not to step on a vine! So we actually require our interns to go barefoot in the fields. A shoeless foot won't destroy a valuable plant."

GARLIC YOGURT TOMATO BITES

From Heritage Hollow Farms

Inspired by Potomac Vegetable Farms

Serves 2 to 4 (or a very hungry 1)

1. Halve the tomatoes and place them on a serving dish, cut side up.

2. Mix the yogurt and garlic in a small bowl, then season with salt.

3. Dollop a small spoonful of the yogurt mixture on top of each tomato half and serve.

*Use a mixture of cherry tomato varieties for a range of tastes and colors.

1 pint cherry tomatoes*
½ cup plain yogurt
2 to 3 garlic cloves, minced
Sea salt

PEAR, CUCUMBER, AND SESAME SLAW

From Potomac Vegetable Farms

Serves 2 to 4

1 pear, peeled, cored, and julienned

1 cucumber, peeled and julienned

3 carrots, peeled and julienned

1 celery stalk, diced

6 scallions, diced

1 tablespoon sesame oil

1 tablespoon sugar

1½ teaspoons apple cider vinegar

1½ teaspoons fresh lemon juice

1½ teaspoons sea salt

1 tablespoon toasted sesame seeds or black sesame seeds

1. Place all the ingredients except the sesame seeds in a large bowl and stir until thoroughly mixed.

2. Sprinkle with the sesame seeds for garnish before serving.

PROSCIUTTO-WRAPPED CANTALOUPE WITH BALSAMIC GLAZE

From Heritage Hollow Farms

Inspired by Potomac Vegetable Farms and Black Oak Holler Farm

Serves 8 to 10

1. Combine the balsamic vinegar and brown sugar in a small saucepan and bring to a simmer over medium-low heat. Simmer for 10 minutes, stirring occasionally. Remove the glaze from the heat and let sit for 1 hour, or until cool.

2. Wrap a piece of prosciutto around a cube of melon. Insert a toothpick to hold it in place and set it on a serving platter. Repeat with the remaining melon and prosciutto. Drizzle with the balsamic glaze. Serve chilled.

1 cup balsamic vinegar

2 tablespoons brown sugar

1 cantaloupe, peeled, seeded, and cut into bite-sized cubes

4 ounces (¼ pound) prosciutto, thinly sliced and cut the same width as the melon cubes

NICHOLS FARM & ORCHARD

MARENGO, ILLINOIS

Vegetables, fruits, and herbs

L loyd Nichols, sixty-nine, won't stop moving. We've just buzzed through his germination house, so packed with basil that an aroma of fresh pesto greets us at the door. Outside, his assistant Carol is watering trolleys brimming with herbs and flowers, purple petunias and spade-leafed sage, potted for sale at Chicago farmers' markets. His youngest son, Todd, rolls past on a John Deere, headed to the strawberry patch, while mechanics Melvin and Ed—straightening bent steel on a cultivator—shout hellos as we breeze through the equipment shed. Lloyd waives to foreman Pablo as we pass his crew, busily bundling spring onions bound for restaurants.

"Let's take the four-wheeler," the gray-haired farmer suggests, hopping into a utility vehicle complete with a roll cage. "That way, we can move a little faster."

I've barely taken my seat before Lloyd hits the accelerator.

Located just outside Marengo, Illinois, a ninety-minute drive northwest of downtown Chicago, Nichols Farm & Orchard is a sprawling four hundred acres of prime, dark earth, with soil the color of triple-chocolate cake. The rich sediments were deposited when glaciers retreated ten thousand years ago, leaving the Great Lakes in their wake. With organic matter at such high levels, it provides a cornucopia of possibilities for area farmers. The opportunity hasn't gone wasted on Lloyd.

Nichols Farm proudly grows *one thousand* different varieties of fruits and vegetables. Rows of radishes flow into fields of rhubarb, bordered by gooseberries and currants, garlic and cabbage. Fronds of asparagus stand at attention like Roman legionnaires, spears planted in unwavering formations, extending for hundreds of feet. Potatoes rub shoulders with fava beans, running parallel to sweet peas stretching ad infinitum. This isn't just a farm. It's a three-credit art class in composition and perspective.

The expansive canvas started out small. A gardener since childhood, Lloyd grew up in Chicago with parents who encouraged him to grow his own vegetables as a boy. Years later, after a stint in the navy that took him to Vietnam in the mid-1960s, he landed a job for TWA loading freight and airplane meals onto passenger planes. It was there he first met Doreen, a flight attendant who made occasional stops in Chicago; after many years of friendship, she at last acquiesced to a date. It wasn't long before the couple married, purchasing a little house with a backyard garden. Or, as it turned out, perhaps it was a backyard garden that came with a little house.

For a young man with a new family, a steady job, and a flourishing vegetable garden, life should have been bliss. And, as Lloyd recalls, it certainly was. But one day a goat changed everything.

Did You Know?

Peak season for fresh asparagus is from mid-April to early June. If foraging for wild varieties, seek out rural roads and slowly drive along old fence rows for best results.

"We had bought that first house, a little place in the suburbs with a tiny plot of land. Naturally, I had a garden, started growing things practically from the day we moved in. But one afternoon as I was driving home, I saw a hand-painted sign: GOATS FOR SALE. So I stopped and bought a nanny goat for my boys." He shrugs, spreading his hands as if to say, "What could I do? I didn't have any choice."

"So everything was going great. We built a little goat shed, even got a buck and had a couple of kid goats. Then one day the homeowners association told me, 'You can't have livestock here, it says so right in the deed.' And do you know, they were right?" He pauses, the frustration as real as if it had happened yesterday and not decades before. "It was all right there, in black-and-white."

Faced with a breach of covenant, Lloyd and Doreen did what any reasonable adults with two small children would do. They packed up their goats, sold the house, and moved out to the country.

"Our thought was 'Hey, let's start a homestead. Let's be sustainable.' Remember, this was the mid-1970s. Inflation was out of control, and everyone was worried about the economy. A lot of people were buying gold." He laughs. "We bought a ten-acre farm instead. I raised a few more goats, a Jersey cow, and a couple of pigs. Then one day I said, 'Well, we've got all this  land, we should grow four acres of vegetables.'" The old farmer leans forward, arching his gray eyebrows. "Four acres of vegetables for one family? In hindsight it was like, 'Let's see how crazy I can be!'"

Did You Know?

According to the USDA, farmers' markets have grown from fewer than 1,800 locations to more than 8,500 nationwide over the past twenty years.

Crazy or not, Lloyd was a natural gardener, and four acres quickly yielded far more than one family could possibly eat. One morning, a friend happened to stop by. Seeing the amazing abundance of vegetables, he offered to take a load to an Evanston farmers' market the following Saturday.

Lloyd, still working full-time for the airline, had never seriously considered selling his vegetables, only growing them for subsistence. But the idea of extra income sounded like a great idea, so after some hurried negotiations they loaded up a truck, and the farmer watched it trundle down the road to Chicago. Later that weekend, his friend returned to the farm. The vegetables were gone, replaced with a plump pocketful of money. "Hey," Lloyd thought to himself. "There might be something to this sustainable farming idea after all."

Progress was particularly sweet when, in the mid-eighties, TWA was purchased by speculative investor Carl Icahn. In short order the company was gutted, and like many of his peers, Lloyd was unexpectedly given severance. He had been farming on evenings and weekends the whole time, but had counted on the airline job to provide for his retirement and financial security. After the dust settled on negotiations, Lloyd received a fraction of what he was originally promised, and the freight handler soon found himself unexpectedly cast into the role of full-time farmer.

Fast-forward thirty-five years. Nichols Farm now attends Chicago-area farmers' markets seven days a week, serving fourteen different locations. Lloyd's sons help run the farm, with the assistance of more than a dozen full-time employees. Nichols has a robust CSA membership, and also provides weekly deliveries to a hundred metro-area restaurants. When one airline closed, it just so happened a farming door opened wide.

But one pickup load of vegetables doesn't turn into fourteen markets overnight, any more than ten acres suddenly becomes four hundred. As it turns out, Lloyd collects farmland like a kid collects baseball cards. He shows me a series of aerial photographs on his wall, displayed in chronological order beginning from 1976.

"This was the original ten," he says, pointing to a large, faded topographic photo with his house in the center. "Look. You can see the first piles of compost, and where we kept the pigs. Now, compare it to this," he says, sidestepping to his right. "Just one year later. Notice any changes?"

It's the same vantage point, with the same house at the epicenter. The difference, however, is startling. Multiple grids of young fruit trees are plainly visible, as well as long, rectangular rows of vegetable beds. Within twelve months, Lloyd and Doreen had demonstrably altered the landscape, converting what had been a decades-old cornfield, yielding only a single crop, into something diversified, something perennial.

The photos stretch on and on, and Lloyd flashes through them like cue cards. In one picture, a handful of acres had been bought in the early 1980s, and in the next, a neighbor who retired had offered more land at a good price. We time-lapse into the mid-nineties, where there's forty acres one year, forty-five the next. The maps on the wall show a gradual but undeniable greening of the landscape, a transformation of fallow, commodity grain fields into geometric patterns of fresh fruits and vegetables. Taking in the whole, it's easy to envision a ripple on a pond, concentric circles expanding from the toss of a single pebble.

Back on the four-wheeler, Lloyd explains that growing a thousand varieties of fruits and vegetables requires constant experimentation, as well as enormous risk tolerance. Rounding a copse of mature apple trees, he points out casualties of the devastating winter, a polar vortex that lashed his fields with wind and snow. Beside budding saplings already setting fruit, a dozen trees stand gray and lifeless.

Lloyd's Farming Wisdom

"When it comes to old farms, you can never tell how good the soil will be. Soil that might have once been spectacular can be eroded away through plowing and human mismanagement. You might look at an old picture and say, 'Wow! Is this really the same land?'"

Did You Know?

Anthropologists believe that Chicago got its name from the Algonquin word *shikaakwa*, which roughly translates to "stinky onion." Before white settlers arrived, the region was named by Native Americans for the wild garlic and ramps that grew along Lake Michigan.

"This is how we learn," he explains, "how we figure out what'll work in our particular climate. This past winter, phew!" He rubs the back of his neck, grimacing at the thought. "We got down to thirty below." "Thirty below zero!" he repeats. "That's the coldest it's ever been in my lifetime."

To mitigate weather liabilities, the farm plants multiple seedlings of the same crop, strategically staggering the plots from one end of the farm to the other. "You never know when you'll get a hailstorm, or heavy rain. Sometimes the weather can be catastrophic on one end of the farm, but you barely know it on the other. This way, we've always got something in season to take to market, no matter how bad the weather gets."

Accounting for Chicago's notoriously windy conditions, young conifers are planted along the edge of each field. The trees will eventually grow into living windbreaks, while simultaneously preventing soil erosion with their roots. Lloyd points to a newly planted sapling the size of a diminutive Christmas tree. Its dark green branches are tipped with tender young needles, a sure sign that the harsh winter has finally retreated.

Farming requires a certain surrender, a concession to wildlife that enjoys fresh produce every bit as much as farmers' market shoppers do. "Yeah, we lose crops to the deer, for sure. Raccoons, too. Even geese." Noting my surprise, he nods emphatically. "You ever see a flock of geese go through a field of spring onions? It's like a lawn mower! They'll wipe you out." Intentionally planting extra—as much as 20 percent more than he thinks he might need—provides a cushion against wildlife damage.

Coming from the rolling highlands of Appalachia, I had no real concept of what hundreds of acres of vegetables might look like. Like most farmers, I keep a modest home garden: a backyard patch of tomatoes and lettuce, sweet corn and watermelons. But nothing had prepared me for the sheer vastness of forty acres of potatoes, or twenty acres of squash, parcels that seemed to stretch beyond the bending horizon. I stand awestruck along the edge of a field of green peppers, epic in size,

losing count as the rows blend into solid stripes of green.

Vegetables on this scale will surely feed thousands of people, and the fact that this is accomplished year after year, decade after decade, speaks to something beyond mainstream economics. The work being done on Nichols Farm implies a currency of faith, ambitions of breadth commensurate with depth.

For the farmer, however, this is just part of the daily scenery. Moments later, he whisks me back to the greenhouse, where eldest son Chad, forty-two, is potting seedlings.

"This was our first big expansion, probably twenty years ago now," Lloyd recalls. "We built it to get an early jump on the season."

Chad sighs, gently shaking his head. "Dad. We built it because Mom kicked you off the porch."

Lloyd stops in his tracks. "No," the farmer insists. "We built it because—"

"Because," his son interrupts good-naturedly, "you had so many seedlings on the sunporch that Mom could barely move."

A small light of memory dawns on the old farmer's face. "Huh? Oh, yeah, I guess that was the reason, wasn't it?"

Chad smiles wordlessly, methodically potting his plants. There's nothing like family, I note to myself, to help straighten out a story.

Out in the parking lot, Lloyd pauses near the edge of a woodlot. "You know," he says, staring up at a century-old white oak bordering the driveway, "these trees here, a lot of farmers would have logged them years ago, made more room for crops. But I've got a little secret. Each year, we harvest enough wild mushrooms from these woods to pay the taxes on the acreage."

His smile is contagious, eyes crinkling at the corners. As he speaks, a childlike note of joy plays across his voice. "We didn't even plant those mushrooms, they just grow there. How can you beat that?"

It takes a great farmer to raise crops without even trying. Lloyd waves a friendly good-bye, and I point my car east, headed toward Chicago. A few miles down the road, there's a FOR SALE sign along the edge of an old soybean farm, and within moments my mind connects the dots. I can hardly wait to see what this farmer does with his next hundred acres.

FRESH LINGUINE WITH SPRING RADISHES AND PEAS

From Nichols Farm & Orchard

Serves 4 to 6

With the crisp crunch of radishes and bright taste of peas, this pasta dish provides the perfect taste of spring. The fresh linguine recipe comes from chef John MacPherson at Foster Harris House in Washington, Virginia, who also contributed his talents to preparing and styling many of the recipes seen throughout these pages.

1. Cook the pasta according to the directions, until al dente. Drain, reserving 1 cup of the cooking liquid.

2. Heat the oil in a large skillet over medium-high heat. Add the scallions, garlic, and pepper flakes. Sauté until softened and fragrant, about 2 minutes.

3. Add the radishes and peas. Cook, stirring occasionally, until soft, about 5 minutes. Season with salt and pepper.

4. Add the pasta and reserved cooking liquid to the pan. Cook until the sauce evenly coats the pasta, about 2 minutes.

5. Toss with the Parmesan and herbs. Serve immediately.

1 pound fresh linguini (Homemade Pasta recipe follows, or use store-bought)

¼ cup olive oil

3 scallions, thinly sliced

2 garlic cloves, thinly sliced

½ teaspoon red pepper flakes

1 pound spring radishes (Easter Egg, French Breakfast, Icicle, etc.), cut lengthwise and thinly slice

6 ounces fresh English peas, shelled

Salt and freshly ground black pepper

½ cup grated aged Parmesan

Chopped fresh herbs (such as parsley, oregano, and marjoram) to taste

HOMEMADE PASTA

From John MacPherson at Foster Harris House

Serves 4 to 6

3½ cups (16 ounces)
unbleached all-purpose
flour

2 large eggs

12 large egg yolks

1 tablespoon olive oil

2 tablespoons milk

1. Mound the flour on a flat surface and make a well in the center, pushing the flour to the sides to create a ring with sides about 1 inch wide. Make sure that the well is wide enough to hold all the eggs without spilling.

2. Pour the eggs and yolks, oil, and milk into the well. Use your fingers to break the eggs up. Still using your fingers, begin turning the eggs in a circular motion, keeping them within the well—don't let them spill over the sides. (This circular motion allows the eggs to gradually pull in flour from the sides of the well; it is important not to mix the flour too rapidly, or your dough will be lumpy.) Keep moving the eggs while slowly incorporating the flour. Using a pastry scraper, occasionally push the flour toward the eggs; the flour should be moved only enough to maintain the gradual incorporation of the flour, and the eggs should continue to be contained within the well. The mixture will thicken and eventually become too tight to keep turning with your fingers.

3. When the dough begins to thicken and starts lifting itself from the surface, use the pastry scraper to incorporate the remaining flour: Lift the flour up and over the dough that's beginning to form, and then cut it into the dough. When the remaining flour from the sides of the well has been cut into the dough, the mixture will be jagged. Bring the dough together with the palms of your hands and form it into a ball. It will look flaky, but it will hold together.

4. Knead the dough by pressing it, bit by bit, in a forward motion with the heels of your hands, rather than folding it over on itself as you would with bread dough. Re-form the dough into a ball and repeat the process several times. The dough should feel moist but not sticky. Let the dough rest for a few minutes while you clean the work surface.

5. Dust the clean work surface with a little flour. Knead the dough again by pushing against it in a forward motion with the heels of your hands. Form the dough into a ball again and knead it again. Keep kneading in this forward motion until the dough becomes silky-smooth. The dough is ready when you can pull your finger through it and the dough wants to snap back into place. The kneading process can take anywhere from 10 to 15 minutes. (Even if you think you are finished kneading, knead it for a few extra minutes; you cannot over-knead this dough. It is important to work the dough long enough to pass the pull test; otherwise, when it rests, it will collapse.)

6. Double-wrap the dough in plastic wrap to ensure that it does not dry out. Let the dough rest for at least 30 minutes and up to 1 hour before rolling it through a pasta machine.* The dough can be made a day ahead, wrapped and refrigerated; bring to room temperature before cooking it.

7. To cook the dough, bring 6 quarts of salted water to a boil. Add the pasta and cook for 1 to 3 minutes, until al dente.

*You can make this without a pasta machine: Just use a rolling pin to roll the dough out to your desired thickness, and then cut it into strips using a sharp knife or pizza cutter.

LAVENDER AND LEMON BALM MINT TEA

From Wild Roots Apothecary

Inspired by Nichols Farm & Orchard

Makes about 1 cup

This herbal tea sings "summer," when you go out in the morning and see all the glistening dew and pluck a few of your favorite herbs for either sun tea or regular tea. Dried herbs can be used during the winter months to help remind you of summer!

1. Place all the herbs in a 1-quart jar. Pour hot water over them and steep for at least 15 minutes for regular tea. To make sun tea, use room-temperature water in a glass jar and place in the sun for a few hours to infuse (room-temperature water will sun-brew faster than cold water would).

2. Add honey and lemon to your liking and enjoy.

1 fresh lavender sprig

1 ounce (about 1 cup loosely packed) fresh lemon balm leaves or 2 teaspoons dried lemon balm

1 ounce (about 1 cup loosely packed) fresh mint leaves or 2 teaspoons dried mint

About 1 cup hot water

Local honey

Fresh lemon juice

3

HAYTON FARMS BERRIES

MOUNT VERNON, WASHINGTON

Organic berries

//////////////////////////////////

Picture a single blueberry, held aloft between finger and thumb, plump and round and dark as indigo, dusted with a fairy breath of azure. Hold it there. Study it from different angles. Sweet with sincerity, robed in pleated skirts, blueberries are our annual summer crush, lovely little heartbreakers puckering for sugar-tart kisses. Plucked from the top of a pint, placed on the tip of the tongue, each berry is a fleeting affair, like a day at the beach where we fall in love ten times in an afternoon. And who wouldn't? Who couldn't? A life without blueberries, after all, is a life without joy.

And so I stand in a forty-acre blueberry field, mountains cascading in the distance, Mount Baker towering majestically snowcapped, and the valley flush with ripe summer fruit. Dionysus, bless my soul. I pop an entire fistful, a dozen lusty beauties picked straight from the bush, sun-warmed and crunchily soft as they tumble across my palate. Scrumptious. Sumptuous. Downright hedonistic. Cheeks puffed like a chipmunk, eyes rolled in sugary euphoria, for five seconds I risk a photo opportunity worthy of social-media blackmail.

But worth it? Oh, yeah. So totally worth it.

"Absolutely," says Angelica Hayton, twenty-nine, a fifth-generation farmer and Pacific Northwest berry maven. "Pick as many as you'd like. We've got about a million right this second."

Seasons bring fleeting moments of abundance, mystical weeks where bushes and trees are laden to breaking with fruit—oftentimes more than can even be picked. Chest-deep in blueberries, each bush adorned with hundreds of perfect clusters, it would be easy to fool myself into thinking the harvest might never end. But the farmer in me knows the day can't last, that these stolen hours must be savored for their succor and sweetness. It's a lesson that Angelica and her father, Robert, sixty-seven, know all too well.

"This farm has been rescued by big harvests," Robert says, "those once-in-a-generation seasons where all the stars align. Perfect crops, perfect prices, perfect weather at harvest time." His voice carries a rolling cadence, a musical lilt worn smooth from decades of hard work in the fields. "For every one great season, though, you've got ten years of tough. I've been farming my whole life, and those odds have stayed pretty steady."

Located in Washington's Skagit Valley, a little more than an hour north of Seattle, the Hayton family has reinvented itself several times over a century and a half, their six-hundred-acre farm growing and shrinking many times over that span. "In 1917," Robert recounts, "my grandfather made a fortune selling cabbage. He'd been a dairyman, but during World War I, cabbage prices soared to a dollar a pound, and around here you could grow one ton per acre. Two thousand dollars an acre," he says meaningfully. "That was a lot of money back then. It pulled him out of years of debt. But they never saw those prices again. Every generation, you see, has to find its own opportunity."

The barnyard is bustling with activity, tractors and trucks traversing the dusty gravels, men hammering rivets into a steel conveyor line. The barns and equipment sheds operate like a timeline, an arc of prosperity interrupted by lean years. An old dairy shed has been converted to a potato-processing room. The cavernous hay barn now shelters farmers' market trucks. Even the old milking parlor has been retrofitted, and a half-dozen farmhands fold berry boxes into cardboard origami.

"Old buildings are the soul of the farm," Robert says reverently. "It's where the spirit resides." We're standing in a venerable dairy parlor, tongue-and-groove boards painted white as milk. The farmer points above his head, where light streams through a wooden ventilation shaft. A sunbeam casts a spotlight across the well-trafficked floor.

"When I was a teenager in the late fifties," he continues, "milk prices were so bad that farms everywhere were going bust. I remember saying to my dad, 'Listen. We've got to get out of dairying. We need to change with the markets, grow something different.'" Robert studies a thick support post of native fir, worn smooth by decades of passing cattle, still splinterless and strong. "And you know what? To my surprise, he did." Smiling, his mustache bristles. "Farmers can

Robert's Farming Wisdom

"At the end of the day, if a farmer has been able to buy land and keep it, that's really what he's got. The land. In farming, you never really have money; if you do, it's here one day and gone the next. For a farmer, land is your equity, your retirement."

adapt, and so can old buildings. Seems a shame to lose either one."

The barn is an appropriate intersection between old and new. Robert's great-grandfather pioneered his way here from Kentucky, forsaking the strife of post–Civil War Reconstruction for an uncertain homestead in the Pacific Northwest. He migrated with his wife in 1875; she rode a mule, and he walked the entire way—more than two thousand miles. Allow me to repeat that last part: He walked two thousand four hundred miles, leading his wife on a bridled mule. And for what? To carve levees into the swampy terrain, hand-shoveling trenches to drain the marsh into arable soil. Robert laughs at the impossibility of it all, the raw determination in the face of nearly insurmountable odds.

"Yeah, those were some brave people, moving all that way to a place they'd never even seen. But change has always been in my family."

He says this matter-of-factly, concessionary, but a weight hangs about his words, a gravitas of time. "When I came back from college, I went straight into farming, thinking I could make a living if I just worked hard enough. I grew pickling cucumbers for many years, and it went pretty well. Then guess what?" He stops, hands in pockets. "All of a sudden, India became a global player. They pay their workers a dollar a day, and I pay my people a hundred."

Robert regards me with weary, crow's-footed eyes. "How do you compete with that? Well," he continues, answering what I thought was a rhetorical question, "if you want to survive, then you adapt. You focus on what can be grown here, crops that *can't* be shipped from China. Like berries, for example."

Enter Angelica. In kindergarten, when her teacher asked what she wanted to be when she grew up, she was the only girl in her class to say "farmer." Like her father, Angelica was raised on the family farm, selling berries from a roadside stand before she was ten. As soon as her sisters were old enough to drive, they loaded the truck each Saturday morning and drove to Seattle's famous Pike Place Market, vending raspberries, strawberries, and blueberries. Eventually, her sisters left the farm for careers elsewhere, but she stayed on, helping her dad in the summers when she came home from college. It was in college where the idea of farming truly struck home—in particular, the idea of farming organically.

Dad balked at the idea. He was proud of his daughter, of course, honored that she'd want to be a farmer like himself. But he had tried to farm organically in the seventies, raising a crop of no-spray raspberries. There were too many pests, he quickly discovered, too much mold and fungi. Too many problems. The experiment had been a disaster, and he swore off organics entirely, at least for his own operation.

Funny, though, how a daughter can bend a father's heart. While Robert continues to farm cauliflower, cucumbers, and potatoes on a large, conventional scale, these days even branding his vegetables and selling directly to Walmart, he found room for his daughter to take over the family's organic berry business. A fastidiously hard worker herself, she soon rewarded his trust. After thirteen years in business, Angelica now coordinates sales to scores of weekly farmers' markets in the Seattle area, a herculean task by any standard.

Did You Know?

Wild blackberry is a truly American food. Grown from New Jersey to Oregon, it is also the state fruit of Alabama.

That many markets, plus a robust wholesale business, requires a tremendous volume of weekly fresh fruit. To spread out the season, she grows multiple varietals of each berry, some early bloomers and others late, some with more sugar and others trending toward tart.

A hundred yards from Interstate 5, cars roaring past at seventy miles per hour, she leads me through acres of trellised blackberry vines bearing onyx-colored fruit every bit as big as my thumb. The grove is now six years old, and if all goes well it will continue to fruit for at least that long again, the berries ripening in a spectrum from white to carmine to ebony.

"These are called Obsidians," she says, offering a large berry for me to sample. Back at home, blackberries grow wild on my Shenandoah Valley farm, and are so mind-warpingly sour that, instinctively, my taste buds recoil at the mere sight. I receive the fruit politely, my mouth already coiled into a

pucker. But this berry is extraordinarily sweet, its purple juice conveying only the subtlest twang of tartness. I enjoy a second, then a third. It's exactly as I'd always hoped a blackberry might taste, sunny and sweet, and unapologetically luscious.

A few fields over, a new crop of black raspberries, on the other hand, requires immediate attention. It's been an unusually dry summer, and acres of young vines, known as canes, are withering in the hot soil. Because there's no water nearby, a truck with a large tank has been brought to the edge of the field, and a bucket brigade of workers has come to the rescue. Robert takes the lead, a sloshing pail in each hand, giving each parched cane a lifesaving drink. As he steps across the rows, watering and administering instructions, Angelica stands beside me, watching.

"My dad is my hero," she says sincerely, her blueberry-hued eyes unblinking. "He's done so much for the family, worked so hard. When I was a kid, we had some impossible years: A terrible flood, the whole farm was underwater for days. Potato prices that hit rock bottom. Like a lot of farmers, Dad had to

Did You Know?

Many farmers, including Hayton Farms Berries, are now able to take WIC and SNAP credits (formerly known as Food Stamps) at farmers' markets, making fresh food more accessible than ever before. Hayton goes an extra step, donating berries leftover at the end of the market to local food banks.

declare bankruptcy, sell off parts of the farm." She purses her lips into a thin line. "But as his daughters, we never knew how bad things really were. He always made us feel rich. Now, years later, he's made it all back." She lowers her voice as her father approaches. "Less than ten percent of all businesses make it through Chapter Eleven. Dad's did."

Back at the farm, we stop at the roadside stand where Angelica and her sisters started their own business as children twenty years earlier. Within moments, a woman pulls off the main road, admiring the offering of red, gold, and periwinkle fruit. Making her selection, she hands money over the counter, happily encumbered with a wide flat of mixed berries. I imagine her fingers will be stained scarlet by the time she gets home.

That's how it all starts, I realize, how a business is born. An honest product, a happy customer. Stick with it, give it some time, and word gets around. *Those guys have the best stuff.* Before you know it, you've got a line.

Later that afternoon, in Bellevue, Washington, that's precisely what I find. I wait patiently behind four customers, each of them leaving with boxes of fresh berries, toting away their treasures with thinly veiled delight. I finally make it to the front and purchase a box of blueberries. The man behind the counter greets me genially.

"Have you tried our berries before?" he asks.

I reflect back to earlier that morning, gorging on blue morsels straight from the bush, and can't help but smile. "Yeah," I reply. "I'm a repeat customer."

Back in my rental car, I nestle the green pint against the armrest, popping berries as I head toward the airport. One berry, then another. The miles disappear beneath my wheels. One berry, now a fourth, I'm pacing myself. One berry, one . . . aww, the hell with it. I cram a whole fistful into my mouth: instant joy and rapture. Funny, how the simplest pleasures are typically the finest. Merging onto the bustling highway, I'm as happy as a kid on summer vacation.

FRESH BERRIES AND CREAM

From Heritage Hollow Farms

Inspired by Hayton Farms Berries

Serves about 3

This dessert is very simple, but incredibly satisfying at peak berry season. The ripe berries make it sweet enough on its own—no added sugar needed.

1 pint raspberries
1 pint blueberries
1 pint blackberries
¼ cup heavy cream, chilled*

1. Combine the berries in a medium bowl. Divide the berry mixture evenly into individual serving dishes.

2. Whip the chilled cream with a whisk for about 30 seconds until just slightly thickened. Drizzle the cream over the berries and serve.

*You can swap the cream for coconut milk to make a dairy-free version.

RASPBERRY BEER COCKTAIL

From Hayton Farms Berries

Serves 3 or 4

¾ cup fresh or frozen raspberries

2 tablespoons sugar

Juice of 1 lemon

Three-and-a-half 12-ounce bottles of beer (pale ale, amber, or wheat), chilled*

½ cup vodka

Lemon and lime slices

1. Muddle the raspberries in the bottom of a drinking glass or mason jar, then add the sugar and lemon juice. Stir together with the beer and vodka.

2. Serve over ice. Garnish with lemon and lime slices, if desired.

*Seek out a local craft brewery and experiment with different flavors.

BLUEBERRY SALSA

From Hayton Farms Berries

Serves 2 to 4

2 cups coarsely chopped blueberries + 1 cup whole blueberries

3 tablespoons chopped fresh cilantro

2 jalapeño chiles, seeded and minced

⅓ cup diced red bell pepper

¼ cup fresh lemon juice

½ teaspoon kosher salt

Try pairing this wonderful berry-filled salsa with the Guacamole from Garcia Organic Farms (page 254).

1. Toss the chopped blueberries, cilantro, chiles, and bell pepper together in a large bowl. Add the whole blueberries, lemon juice, and salt.

2. Serve immediately, or cover and chill for 8 hours to allow the flavors to really meld.

4

D-TOWN FARM

DETROIT, MICHIGAN

Vegetables, honey, and compost

On the southern edge of River Rouge Park, just off Warren Avenue, an abandoned grocery looms dark and vacant. The facade has been stripped of its insignia, and where neon letters once glowed, shadowy imprints now resemble faded bruises. The empty parking lot simmers beneath a relentless summer sun, motor oil stains opalescent, storm drains clogged with sticks and soda bottles. Where River Rouge ends, urban Detroit begins, stretching for miles along concrete corridors flanked with fast-food restaurants, payday loan fronts, and auto-parts stores. Driving west from downtown Detroit, the view blurs into a gradient of rusting chain link and sun-bleached vacancy posters.

A right turn onto Outer Drive, a soft left onto Joy, and I find myself ducking through a woven wire fence, a gap I surely would have overlooked if I hadn't already known my destination. A small sign blooms from a treadless tire, hand-painted stripes of yellow, green, and red welcoming me to D-Town. It's early morning, and my soles track dew as I step from a buffer of thick grass onto a neatly mulched pathway. I find Aba Ifeoma and Ras Andrew Diaminah in the greenhouse, where they're discussing a mystery.

"Something killed a snake last night," Ras says somberly, "and we're trying to find out how a predator got inside the greenhouse. See, we encourage beneficial species on the farm, and snakes are helpful at keeping pests away.

"We put up this fence to keep the deer out, which works great. But now the foxes and coyotes can't get in, and we're overrun with groundhogs and rabbits! Nature teaches you quickly, you've gotta have balance in the system."

But last night something slipped in and killed one, which is a shame." He speaks with a subdued, reverent air, almost as though he's lost a friend. "Little details make a difference, you know? We need all the allies we can get."

I've been in Detroit for only a few days, but I already sense his meaning. In a city where one block lies in rubble while the next shows hints of restoration, alliances are being reinvented out of necessity. Garter snakes notwithstanding, however, one might wonder where these allies will come from; Detroit's population has decreased by one million people in the past fifty years, and the impact has been palpable. I spent the morning navigating streets of windowless, abandoned buildings downtown, and I mention the vacant grocery store less than a mile away.

"Yes, the last of the supermarkets pulled out in 2007," says Aba, acting director of D-Town. "And when I say all of them, I mean all." Her soft tone can't mask the passion behind her words. "We used to have six different major grocery chains. Now we have zero. Zero groceries, and that leaves few options for people to buy fresh produce. But look around," she adds, brightening. "We're making big strides to change that."

Exit supermarkets; enter D-Town. A seven-acre urban farm nestled into the northwest corner of Detroit's largest park, D-Town Farm was conceived by community leaders who saw the trend of corporations abandoning their city and stepped in to help solve the problem. The organization, dubbed the Detroit Black Community Food Security Network, was founded by Malik Yakini, a former public-school administrator of the year. Growing from the community it

intends to serve, the group emphasizes the critical importance of black leadership and local role models serving local needs. The ultimate goal? Agricultural self-reliance and food justice for the city, fostered by robust community participation.

"People call Detroit a 'food desert,'" Aba continues, "a place where gas stations are the only place you can buy groceries. But if I had a wish, it would be that gas stations could only sell gas, and food would only come from farms." She smiles sweetly. "I'll even make them a deal: If they'll promise not to sell candy bars, D-Town will promise not to sell gasoline."

The reality of eating dinner from a gas station floors me. How could a family hope to raise a healthy child on such meager options?

Standing in the middle of the farm, I hear traffic on the side streets, airplanes roaring overhead. There's no doubt we're surrounded by a major city. Yet something here is different from most towns in America, where a supermarket or greengrocer is rarely more than a few blocks away. In Detroit, gas stations have been left to fill this void, offering soda pop and potato chips for nourishment. It seems if there was ever a time to push back, to value compost over concrete, then Detroit's moment has arrived.

Did You Know?
Composted, it takes a banana peel three to four weeks to revert to soil. A plastic bottle? 450 years.

"Soil," says Kadiri Sennefer, chief of composting operations at the farm. Kadiri lingers over the word, savoring the sound. "Don't mistake and call this 'dirt.'" He cups his hands beneath freshly screened compost, holding it out for me to smell. "To me, 'dirt' is a cuss word. It means something unproductive, nonbeneficial." He allows the dark soil to tumble from his fingertips. "Dirt is something people walk on, but soil is fruitful. This is where fertility begins."

The earth in his hands, once heaps of moldering vegetables and wood chips, now smells like a healthy forest: richly mineralized, oaky, complex. Several times a week Kadiri flips compost piles the size of automobiles, incorporating wood chips as he goes. This action mixes carbon and oxygen to offset ammonia and pathogens, fostering a hotbed of microorganisms that cook the mixture to temperatures exceeding 150 degrees Fahrenheit. On cool mornings, steam wafts from the compost like bread fresh from the oven. D-Town manufactures dump-truck loads of excess fertilizer each year, nutrient-rich soil that will be shared with other urban farms around the region.

Following the mission of food self-reliance, this large-scale composting has all the makings of a closed-loop system. "You mentioned those abandoned city lots? That soil is terribly polluted," Aba explains. "Lead, toxic chemicals, you name it. Our mentor Will Allen kept pressing us to create compost, not buy it. So in 2011 we started making it, and in a big way. We visited Allen's farm, Growing Power, in Milwaukee, and took his composting classes. The following summer he came to D-Town and helped us get started."

There's an old saying that, when the student is ready, the teacher will appear. Allen, a former professional basketball player and the recipient of a MacArthur Genius Grant, has made frequent visits to the farm, providing guidance along the way. These days, D-Town has working relationships with Wayne County's forestry department for a steady source of carbon-rich wood chips, as well as Forgotten Harvest, a not-for-profit that salvages vegetables from supermarkets outside the city and trucks them into Detroit for at-risk families. Vegetables that are past their prime end up with Kadiri—truckloads of tomatoes, squash, and lettuce, providing nutrients that are slowly recycled into compost.

The words *agricultural self-reliance* look lovely on paper, mission-statement poetry if ever there was. Yet, putting these words into action—prioritizing deeds over talk—cultivates a poetry of muscle, soil, and steel. Kadiri strikes his hands—*smack, smack*—and the final grains of compost tumble from his palms. Moments later he heads back into his morning routine, a glinting pitchfork balanced neatly over one shoulder.

Like many great ideas in the concept stages, D-Town experienced several years of false starts before finding traction. The original farm started on a quarter-acre plot near Detroit's east side, on a vacant housing lot near a 4-H club. A year later, when the space was bought by a developer, they relocated to a half acre owned by a local church. After two more years of searching for a permanent location, they finally secured a ten-year license via the Parks and Recreation Department. For the rental price of one dollar a year, River Rouge Park became their new home.

Dating back to six original farms, the thirteen-hundred-acre River Rouge parcel was purchased by the city in the 1920s. Officials promised the space would rival Central Park in splendor and be an urban oasis of recreation and serenity. After several decades, however, River Rouge Park began a slow, steady

Did You Know?

Detroit is the oldest city in America beyond the original thirteen colonies and was founded in 1701. The Detroit River lends the city its name, an Americanization of the French word for "the straight."

decline. State-of-the-art swimming pools, built to court a potential Olympic bid, have been empty for years. Brambles choke the once-spacious bike paths, and baseball fields languish waist-deep in swaying grass. Driving through the park earlier that morning, along a winding three-mile road, the expansive space was eerily unpopulated: I observed a solitary jogger and a few pedestrians walking their dogs. River Rouge seems to be a park in search of its people.

Over the years, officials designated a large portion of the acreage as a nursery, supplying young trees to the city of Detroit. Called the Walter Meyers Tree Nursery, this is where D-Town found its home, two acres at first, then another two, then finally three more. All told, the farm currently has access to seven prime acres, bounded on three sides by the tree nursery.

On the grounds of D-Town, it's easy to feel the resonance of the original park. Pathways are marked with educational signposts, and seventy-year-old cottonwoods offer shade to passersby. Apple and pear, mulberry and cherry trees punctuate the open spaces, providing an understory to red oak, locust, and shagbark hickory. Raised beds brim with young salad greens, and hoop houses are filled with peppers and tomatoes. With the sweet smells of fruit and honeysuckle permeating the air,

it's understandable that visitors would seek sanctuary here, reconnecting with soil so often armored by sidewalks and pavement.

A changing landscape demands not only new alliances but also new ways to communicate, and for a generation raised exclusively within city limits, agriculture must seem like a foreign language. For thirty-year-old

Ras, it was a trip to Ghana that galvanized an interest in sustainable farming, expanding his cultural horizons. Spending time with a friend there, they devoted part of each day in the garden cultivating food that would later end up on the dinner table. To Ras, gardening in Ghana at first seemed like a foreign enterprise, far removed from the urban landscape of his Kalamazoo childhood. Gradually, however, the idea of transplanting his knowledge back in Michigan began to take root, and he found a job working at D-Town.

In the greenhouse, Ras sits on the wooden edge of a raised bed, weeding a succulent row of mixed lettuces. "This is intended as a demonstration farm, a place where people can put in sweat equity. Learn what it really takes to grow healthy food." A day on the farm, Ras explains, is meant to inspire, reviving ancestral traditions lost across the generations. Collaborating with the farmers offers practical experience to those who might have never planted a seed.

"I mean, success never comes overnight, you know what I'm saying? When all this started in 2006, there was no funding, no grant money. People made sacrifices of time and energy—and money, of course—to make this happen. Folks gave whatever they could."

In 2012, the W. K. Kellogg Foundation, a philanthropy group emphasizing healthy child development and racial equality, recognized the importance of their work and became a major funder. The USDA soon followed, offering support for the Food Warriors program, an educational outreach to area school children. Deeply grateful for this support, Ras also envisions a time when these expanded programs will be fiscally self-reliant, through ever-increasing vegetable sales and composting operations.

"That's one of our goals, and we're moving in that direction. Financial independence for all our projects . . . yeah, every farm wants that. But even when we get there, we see turning it right back into the farm. Hiring more people, extending our educational programs."

Detroit's motto is *Speramus meliora; resurget cineribus*: "We hope for better things; it shall rise from the ashes." Ras Diaminah's personal motto is no less auspicious: *Manifest*.

"I got this tattoo on my right arm, my working arm, to remind me about what's possible, what one person can do." Soft spoken and pensive, he considers his words before continuing. "This kind of farming, it entails a certain relationship with the earth. Take GMOs, for example—genetically modified organisms. When you take all that we *don't* know about them, and combine it with what we do know, the picture's pretty clear. Farming that way, there are ill effects on our soil, our water table. Increased weed and pest resistance. And that's not even accounting for the economics." He studies me plainly, the face of a man who has weighed the facts and chosen his path. "That whole vibe is just bad news. With organic farming,

we might have to give more of ourselves. But in the end, we get more back."

Outside, a flowering buckeye is in full bloom, thick with pink blossoms and honeybees knitting the air. It's an exquisite blue morning, and saddlebags of pink pollen are clearly visible on the bees' legs, destined to become buckeye honey back at their hive.

"This is a prime example of how things work around here," Aba says. "When we started out, we knew we wanted bees—needed bees—but we didn't have anyone to raise them. Little did I know, there was a local beekeeper who kept asking Malik, 'When are you going to send me someone to train?' So eventually, I volunteered." A look of wonder brightens her face. "What did I know about keeping bees? Not the first thing. But I was patient and willing to learn. Now, look. We have bees."

She pauses, contemplating the hives in the distance. "You know, we're not out to feed the entire city. It's really about everybody growing, everybody learning *to* grow. Not becoming dependent on any one entity to supply our food." She spreads her palms, gesturing, I presume, to the phantom grocery stores that have pulled out of the city. "We've seen that model. It doesn't work."

I need no convincing. When human spirit is surrendered for productivity, sustainability becomes measured by rubble heaps. In a city where Henry Ford famously wished for only a pair of hands—not the person they belonged to—an emerging economy is quietly rewriting old rules. Abundance, we're learning, is something to be shared, not hoarded.

Speramus meliora; resurget cineribus. We hope for better things; it shall rise from the ashes. Long live Detroit, championed by the optimists, the indefatigable.

Aba's Farming Dream

"There's a vacant lot on every block in Detroit. My vision is to see a community garden in every neighborhood, a way for people to reconnect, not just with their food, but with one another. Lord knows, we don't do that enough."

TOMATO SAUCE FROM SCRATCH

From D-Town Farm

Makes about 4 cups of sauce

Serve this sauce over pasta (try making your own from the recipe on page 32), roasted spaghetti squash, or anything else you like.

1. Bring a large pot of water to a boil. Fill a large bowl halfway with ice and water. Place the tomatoes in the boiling water for 30 to 45 seconds. Remove and immediately place in the ice-water bath. Take the tomatoes out of the ice water and peel off the skins. Working over a strainer set in the sink, squeeze the tomatoes and discard the seeds and excess water.

2. Heat the oil and salt in a large skillet over high heat. Add the tomatoes, basil, and oregano. Lower the heat to a simmer and cook for about 45 minutes, stirring occasionally. (The time it takes will depend on your desired consistency; allow less time for a chunkier sauce and more time to allow the tomatoes to break down for a thinner sauce.) Taste for seasoning and adjust if necessary before serving.

4 pounds ripe tomatoes

2 tablespoons cold-pressed olive oil

Pinch of kosher salt

Handful of fresh basil, chopped

Handful of fresh oregano, chopped

FULL-FLAVORED COLLARD GREENS

From D-Town Farm

Serves 4 to 6

1 pound collard greens, chopped

1 turnip, diced

2 tablespoons olive oil

1 medium onion, chopped

1 red bell pepper, seeded and chopped

2 garlic cloves, finely chopped

1 tablespoon chopped fresh dill, or to taste

1 teaspoon red pepper flakes, or to taste

1 teaspoon ground cumin, or to taste

Salt and freshly ground black pepper

1 tablespoon apple cider vinegar

2 cups vegetable stock or water

1 tomato, seeded and chopped

1. Bring a large pot of water to a boil and blanch the collard greens and turnip for 3 minutes.* Drain, rinse, and set aside.

2. Heat the oil in a large pot over medium heat. Add the onion and sauté until slightly softened, then add the bell pepper, garlic, dill, pepper flakes, and cumin, and season with salt and pepper. Cook until the onions begin to brown. Add the collard greens and turnip and cook for another 2 to 3 minutes, stirring occasionally.

3. Mix the vinegar with the stock and add it to the pot. Cover and bring to a simmer. Cook until the greens are tender, about 20 minutes. (Note: The longer you cook them, the softer, and less nutritious, they will be.)

4. Garnish with the chopped tomato and serve.

*See page 292 for a guide to blanching.

ROASTED VEGGIES

From Heritage Hollow Farms

Inspired by local, organic vegetable farms everywhere

Makes as much or as little as you want

Roasting is a wonderful method for cooking fresh, organic, locally grown produce. The flavors of the vegetables intensify when you roast them, especially compared to boiling or steaming, which dilutes the taste.

1. Preheat the oven to 375°F.

2. Slice, cube, halve, or wedge a vegetable or a variety of vegetables listed above. Lightly toss in your choice of oil and sea salt.

3. Roast in a single layer in a large rimmed baking pan for about 20 minutes (winter squashes may need 45 to 60 minutes). Root vegetables are done when tender; Brussels sprouts and cauliflower are done when lightly golden brown. Check about halfway through cooking time and toss to evenly roast.

Sweet potatoes or yams

Turnips

Brussels sprouts

Cauliflower

Winter and/or summer squashes

Carrots

Cherry tomatoes

Coconut oil, olive oil, unsalted butter, bacon fat, or lard

Sea salt*

TIPS:

- Roasted sweet potatoes pair well with avocados—try mashing some avocado and using it as a dip!
- Brussels sprouts and bacon taste amazing together.
- Cut an acorn or delicata squash in half and roast it halfway, then fill the cavity with pastured pork sausage and finish baking.

*Check out the wonderful J.Q. Dickinson Salt Works, a seventh-generation salt-making family based in West Virginia: jqdsalt.com

5

OZARK FOREST MUSHROOMS

SALEM, MISSOURI

Shiitake and oyster mushrooms

⁘

I'm three hours southwest of St. Louis, deep in the heart of a thousand-acre forest, and there's a river in the middle of the road. I study the map in my lap. No mistake: The route has been transected, a silvery expanse of water flowing between me and the road reemerging on the distant bank. It's not the first time I've splashed through a ford, but navigating a river would undoubtedly void my rental policy with Enterprise. Who knew that hunting mushrooms could be so difficult?

Fortunately, moments later, Dan and Henry Hellmuth come to my rescue. "I think you missed a turn," Dan says, a native Missourian with a ready smile. He spins his four-wheeler in the opposite direction, pointed back into the dense woods. "Follow us, we'll show you the way. Nicola's ready to get picking."

It's been a wet spring, and the fungus is popping. Nicola McPherson, fifty-seven, moves briskly, hands floating over her mushroom logs, picking shiitakes as neatly as a harpist plucks notes. "Normally, we have to soak the logs to get them to fruit," she explains, "but this spring, with all the rain, it's been steady volunteers. Look, over there. The logs are just bursting with them."

Indeed, the forest is a smorgasbord of fungus. Four-foot oak logs are stacked in all directions, each of them thick with soft brown mushrooms, so many that it would take an entire day to harvest them all. "We've got twenty thousand logs out here," Nicola says, tucking a tendril of gray hair behind her ear as she pauses. "My first year, back in 1990, I started out with maybe fifty. We've grown slowly, building our markets along with our experience."

Twenty thousand logs. Nicola says it so matter-of-factly, so nonchalantly, that the accomplishment might easily go unappreciated. But this is a colossal effort, and the visual proof is stunning. We're standing in a labyrinth of logs. Some are teepeed against wire trellises; others recline like sunbathers beneath the somnolent shade of the white pines. Hundreds are crisscrossed like Lincoln Logs, stacked beneath a canopy of black shade cloth. Even more are stair-stepped up the hillside, a twisting maze of logs and mushrooms that gradually blends into the thick forest.

A half-hour drive from Salem and the closest cell phone reception, it's easy to see how someone might get lost out here in the Ozarks. Perhaps even on purpose.

"My dad bought this property back in the 1950s," Dan explains. "You know . . . in case of a nuclear holocaust." His voice carries only the slightest notes of humor and apology, having lived a cultural history largely unknown to younger generations. "The Cold War was a different time. Growing up

like I did in St. Louis, we felt like we had a big target on our backs. So, when Dad bought acreage all the way down here, it actually wasn't the craziest idea at the time."

It doesn't seem like a crazy idea now, either. The farm is achingly beautiful, with gin-clear water flowing above caramel-colored rocks, catalpa and hemlock dipping green limbs across the gently ambling river. Known as the Sinks, the area is famous for canoeing and camping, karst geology responsible for rivers that disappear into caves only to reemerge some distance downstream. This part of Missouri is so sparsely populated that, when an F-15 crashed in 2007 (the pilot ejected safely), the federal government couldn't locate the plane; they relied on locals to point them to the wreckage. But it's precisely this solitude that's allowed Nicola to grow authentic forest-raised mushrooms, as well as offer a retreat hundreds of miles south of the maddening crowds.

A spring-fed lake pools at the foot of a wooded mountain slope, and a small cottage rests along the shore, a deck built just above the tranquil water. "After Dan's parents passed away, we realized we had more housing than we needed. So we did some renovations and created a guest cottage." She laughs. "It's like us, nothing too fancy. But it's a nice space for the people who want to visit the farm, a chance to find a small escape."

A hummingbird buzzes our way, defying gravity as it taps invisible brakes, floating stationary in midair. Only feet away, it seems intent on studying me, a sentinel appraising an unfamiliar visitor. Moments later, it dashes away on business of its own. Nicola watches it go.

"We've got so many hummingbirds here. And owls. And whip-poor-wills. Have you ever seen a whip-poor-will?" Her eyes light up at the mention. "Strange little birds, only come out at night. The head of an owl, the body of a pigeon. And what a voice!"

A western England transplant now living in rural Missouri, Nicola knows a little something about voices. Her British accent

Nicola's Rural Wisdom

"I think a lot of people are afraid to ever be by themselves, completely away from other people. But being alone every once in a while is important—it helps you remember to like yourself."

is mellifluous, with a polished cadence that brings to mind magical nannies who drift into town on umbrellas. She met Dan strictly on chance, one of two Americans visiting her university on his study abroad program. Long-distance relationships are hard to keep, especially from St. Louis to Bristol, so it wasn't long before she made the move to the States. A daughter and son—Henry, who now works on the farm—soon followed.

Her education quickly landed her a job at the Missouri Botanical Garden. But several times a month, as the family traveled back and forth between St. Louis and the Ozarks, something about the remote woodland property began to speak to her.

"Of course, I come from a farming background myself," Nicola recounts. "Where I grew up, it's surrounded by farms, and I was always raising something: Vegetables, goats, you name it. So when I saw all this land, I just got to thinking, 'Maybe there's something more we could do, something other than just the occasional timber harvest, or making hay in the pastures.' That's really how the whole thing started, just finding something that fit in with the natural landscape."

Shiitakes practically suggested themselves. The environment is an ideal mushroom habitat, with sustainably sourced oak limbs—otherwise typically burned for firewood—readily available from local logging operations. Mushroom logs must always be from freshly felled timber to ensure that competing fungi haven't already colonized the wood. Each winter, after a delivery of fresh limbs, Nicola's crew spends many weeks drilling thumb-size holes into the oak, packing them with mushroom spores, then capping them with wax. If all goes well, the logs become colonized with white mycelium, which are the vegetative "roots" of the mushrooms. Only then, when the conditions are perfect, will the wood fruit with shiitakes bursting through the bark, a dozen lovely mushrooms at a time.

Sometimes, however, perfection requires a little assistance. For shiitake logs, submerging them in water until the wood is fully saturated serves as an on-and-off switch for farmer and fungi alike. On Nicola's farm this job falls to David, an employee of fifteen years, who soaks the tree limbs in large, galvanized water troughs. The old saying goes "form follows function," and it's no accident that David sports biceps the diameter of the oak logs themselves. Goateed and barrel-chested, he looks every part a tree-logger-turned-mushroom-logger. With one hand, he positions a log with the grace of a baseball player taking a practice swing. I jokingly ask him how far he could toss one.

"Thirty feet," he suggests. "Maybe farther?"

I believe him.

Hoisting one myself, I decide it weighs every

Farm Humor

"I always joke, 'Dan's a "fun-gi," so that makes me a "fun girl," right?'" Nicola pauses awkwardly. "Okay, so maybe it's not that funny. Mushroom jokes are hard to come by, and that's no shiitake."

ounce of forty pounds. By contrast I pick a mushroom, cupping it in my hand, marveling at the difference. I had never considered how weightless they truly are, little more than the heft of a bird's feather. Nicola's weekly harvest is three hundred pounds; with each shiitake weighing a fraction of an ounce, I wonder how long it must take to pick, pack, and deliver that much product. Studying the mushroom, I also began to wonder what a fresh, raw shiitake tastes like.

The Japanese speak of a fifth taste, something beyond sweet, sour, salty, and bitter: umami. Best described as pleasantly savory, it's small coincidence that, like the word, shiitakes also originated in Japan. I bite into the mushroom, and while the texture is undeniably meaty, the taste is something different entirely: mellow and woody, reminiscent of the smell of freshly raked autumn leaves. The lightest hint of salt, the slightest note of mineral, a whisper of cracked peppercorn. I find myself savoring the mild aftertaste. Searching for an apt description, it is as though I'd just tasted the forest itself.

Nearby, Henry is busy at work filling boxes. A recent graduate of the University of Missouri's nascent sustainable agriculture program, the twenty-two-year-old speaks thoughtfully as he picks. "Sustainable farming, big ag, local production . . ." he trails off, and the words linger a moment between us. "You know, all the trendy catch phrases. It's a confusing time right now, and I'm actually living it. I grew up with all these words. I can only imagine how hard it is for a customer to understand it."

A thick blanket of pine needles covers the forest floor, softening sounds, and Henry's voice seems to drop accordingly, as though we're two students whispering in a library. "Obviously, my mom has a successful business here, and for our family it's genuinely sustainable. But I just graduated from a major university, a place that happens

to be funded by industrial agriculture companies. If you're a kid coming from a family that plants corn and soybeans for a living, what kind of farming do you think your parents are going to teach you?" He regards me with inscrutable eyes. "Let me put it this way: For the most part, it wasn't traditional farm kids who signed up for sustainable agriculture classes."

He stacks four boxes and carries them to the end of the row. "But it's not like I don't appreciate their side, too; I see both sides of the argument. In college, professors always asked, 'How are we going to feed the world?'" The corners of his mouth dip into a pensive frown. "I wouldn't say that's the right question to be asking, but it does make me wonder about other issues. Food accessibility, for example. Sure, technically industrial agriculture can 'feed the world.' But are we growing enough *good* food? Nutritious food?" Henry spreads his hands.

"Yeah, what we're doing on this farm is great. And I believe in it. When it comes to feeding the rest of the world, though, I keep coming up with more questions than answers."

I help load boxes into their van, shiitake and oyster mushrooms packed floor to ceiling, bound for farmers' markets and restaurants in St. Louis. It's early afternoon; the day has flown by, and it's now time to go. Dan has left ahead of us, and I follow Nicola and Henry in my rental car, navigating gullied dirt roads through the dark forest, doused in shadow even with the sun high above. About a mile or so from the farm, Nicola's van comes to a sudden halt, and she pops her head from the driver's-side window.

"Would you like to see where the river comes through the mountain?"

Would I! Moments later, pants rolled to the knees, Henry and I wade into Sinking Creek, crayfish and sculpins darting

Did You Know?

Beyond Missouri, there are now more than fifty major universities offering degrees in Sustainable Agriculture or related fields; including institutions such as Florida, Iowa State, Kansas State, Montana, Ohio State, Penn State and Virginia Tech.

around our bare feet. As promised, the river flows through an arched tunnel of solid rock, perhaps twenty feet wide and two hundred feet to where daylight floods the distant entrance. Henry reaches into the crystal water, retrieving a smooth, rounded stone.

"I've got a cousin who can skip one all the way through the tunnel," he says. Cocking his arm, he sends the stone whirling into the darkness. Twelve, perhaps fourteen skips; the momentum ends roughly halfway down the tunnel. To make it all the way seems like an impossible task.

Now it's my turn. I find a promising rock, round as a shiitake cap. The missile skips five times before clumsily torpedoing beneath the water. *Kerplunk*.

Henry points skyward, toward the top of a hill forty feet above us, a sheer rock face freckled with asters and wild daisy. "Up there, that's where my grandparents are buried." He absently skips another stone, his expression distant. "It's a beautiful view once you reach the summit. Oh, and see that ledge?" he adds, pointing to a narrow outcropping halfway up the rock face. "When the water's running high enough, we jump from those rocks. Sounds fun, right?"

I study the jump, the deep-plunge pool below, and wonder for how many centuries delighted, yawping Missourians have cannonballed from the heights. Part of me wants to scale the sunny precipice, stepping into midair, comforted by the knowledge that the water will catch me. But today the dunkings are for Dave and his logs; we have a schedule to keep. A few minutes later, back in the car, the dirt road turns to pavement. Before me, the rearview mirror fills with gathering wilderness.

Did You Know?

Translated from Japanese, *shii* is the species of tree on which these fungi were originally cultivated, and *také* means mushroom.

ASIAN MUSHROOM SOUP

From Ozark Forest Mushrooms

Serves 2 to 4

This soothing soup from *The Ozark Mushroom Feast* cookbook is wonderful for when you're feeling under the weather, since it's full of nutritious ingredients such as ginger, lemongrass, and mushrooms that can aid in healing.

1. Soak the mushrooms in warm water for 20 minutes. Drain the mushrooms, reserving the soaking liquid, then remove any mushroom stems. Slice the mushrooms and set aside.

2. Combine the mushroom soaking liquid, stock, lemongrass, ginger, and cilantro in a large saucepan. Bring to a boil over medium-high heat, then lower the heat and simmer for 30 minutes.

3. Remove the lemongrass, ginger, and cilantro. Return the stock to a boil, then add the mushrooms, scallions, soy sauce, rice wine, and the noodles, if using. Cook until the mushrooms are heated through.

4. Taste the soup and add a pinch of salt if desired. Serve hot.

*Available from Ozark Forest Mushrooms at ozarkforest.com.

1 ounce dried shiitake mushrooms*

Warm water for soaking mushrooms

3 cups chicken or vegetable stock

Two 5-inch pieces fresh lemongrass

One ½-inch piece fresh ginger, peeled and thinly sliced

4 fresh cilantro sprigs

4 scallions, chopped

2 tablespoons shiitake mushroom soy sauce*

3 tablespoons rice wine or mirin

Somen, soba, or rice noodles, optional

Sea salt, optional

PESTO SHIITAKE SAUCE

From Ozark Forest Mushrooms

Serves 4 to 6

1 to 2 tablespoons unsalted butter or olive oil

1 pound fresh shiitake mushrooms, stemmed and sliced

2 garlic cloves, peeled and crushed

1 large bunch fresh basil, stemmed and chopped, or 1 tablespoon dried basil

1 tablespoon unbleached all-purpose flour

1 cup milk or half-and-half

Salt and freshly ground black pepper

This recipe was originally featured in *The Ozark Mushroom Feast*. Serve on its own as a side dish or over your favorite pasta (try the Homemade Pasta on page 32) and cheese.

1. Heat the butter in a large skillet over medium heat. Add the mushrooms and garlic and cook, stirring, until the liquid from the mushrooms has reduced, about 10 minutes. Add the basil and stir briefly.

2. Sprinkle in the flour and stir until evenly distributed, then gradually stir in the milk until a thick, creamy sauce forms. Season with salt and pepper before serving.

TIP:

You can often find lemongrass and ginger available from local farmers. If you can't, ask one if they'd be willing to grow them next season!

6

LAGIER RANCHES

ESCALON, CALIFORNIA

Organic almonds and fruit

———

Boysenberry's my favorite," John says, his blue eyes twinkling as our conversation turns to desserts, pie in particular. "So when it came time to convert the farm to organics, I started out with berries. It might not have been my most successful venture, but I sure enjoyed eating them." He grins behind a robust Howard Taft mustache, chuckling at the memory. "Sometimes plans don't work out. But growing what you love . . . that makes the hard work seem a little easier."

An hour and twenty minutes east of San Francisco, John Lagier, fifty-eight, and his partner, Casey Havre, raise certified organic almonds, cherries, grapes, and oranges on his fourth-generation farm near Escalon, California. It's a cloudless blue morning, and the temperature is already beginning to soar. Daily highs of 105 degrees Fahrenheit are not uncommon here, and this mid-April day appears to be no exception. In the shade of an equipment shed, John works on his tractor, knuckles smeared black with lithium grease.

"The transmission gave out yesterday," he explains, "but at least it still goes in reverse." Hand shading his eyes, he squints into the dark recesses of the differential. "It's always something, you know? That's just the way it is around here, your schedule constantly changing around. We're adapting a small tractor to do the work until the other's repaired. One thing's for sure,"

he adds, wiping his hands with a red shop rag. "Farming might drive you crazy, but you'll never get bored."

"Around here" happens to be California's Northern San Joaquin Valley, acreage where John and his family have farmed since his great-grandfather relocated from Missouri in the 1870s. Essentially a dry inland sea filled with rich alluvial sediments, the valley is the beneficiary of millions of years of mountain erosion, minerals carried by eons of snowmelt and rainfall. Fifty miles wide and nearly 450 miles long—an area roughly the size of West Virginia—the expansive, flat valley produces more than 230 different crops each year, comprising nearly 10 percent of the country's food. Almonds are no exception, where six thousand farmers grow 1.9 billion pounds each year, equating to a half pound of nuts for every woman, man, and child in the United States.

The region has recently suffered a multiyear drought, and while driving in from San Francisco, the contrasts couldn't have been more stark. Interstate 580 is an arrow's shot from the bay to the valley, a mist-shrouded, winding ascent through sculpted green hills, easily doubling for *The Lord of the Rings* B-roll footage. Cresting a final ridge, however, the verdant topography yields to a vast, hazy expanse, sepia-toned and sere. This valley is dependent on wells and irrigation: Annual rainfall only reaches twenty inches at best, far less than the dry, thirsty soil requires. Pulling off the interstate, a cloud of dust boiled behind me as I cut a wake toward John's farm.

Now, we pass beneath the limbs of lush cherry trees, immature fruit hanging in green clusters. Not ripe for another month, the grove is irrigated through drip tape that snakes along the root tops, administering a slow trickle of cool, nourishing water.

"It was a hot, dry winter," John recalls, "and our season is running behind. Like these cherries." He turns a green cluster in his calloused hand, the fruit more closely resembling tiny green apples than succulent red fruit. The farmer considers.

"A lot of orchards use accelerant sprays, pushing the harvest along faster. While they're at it, they'll be spraying for leaf mites, and using herbicides to kill the grass under the trees." He releases the unripened fruit, and it disappears into the canopy, instantly camouflaged. "As an organic farmer, it takes a lot more labor, more attention to what's happening at certain times of the year. And when these cherries come on, we have to really jump."

Halfway down the row Casey beckons, turning over a cherry leaf.

"Check this out." The underside of the leaf is dotted with tiny black insects and glistens with a clear, sticky glaze. "These are cherry aphids, a real pest for us, but the ants actually 'farm' them. Yeah," she affirms, noting my quizzical stare, "it sounds like science fiction. The aphids make a sweet nectar out of the sap—this gooey stuff—and the ants come along behind and harvest it. To defend the aphids from predators, the ants wrap the leaves around them like a shield." She breaks the leaf from the twig, and casts it aside. "Of course it's bad for the trees, because when the leaves are curled, they can't photosynthesize. Since we're organic, instead of spraying, we go through by hand each spring, picking out the infested ones."

What a job. Each tree typically has dozens of colonized leaves, and there are hundreds of trees in the orchard. It takes two workers an entire week of culling to make an impact on the pests.

Casey's Farm Tradition

"My grandmother always said to make a wish on the first cherry of the year. You get one wish, and that's it! So each year, I make a wish on a cherry."

Still, as we reach the end of the row, the challenge pales compared to the legion of young almonds facing us, forty acres of newly planted trees. Thousands of young saplings are gridded across the horizon, rooted into supple, mounded rows.

The variety is called Independence, bred to have self-pollinating blossoms, eliminating the need for honeybees to be trucked onto the farm. Even so, I notice bees happily buzzing beneath the shade of the trees, gathering pollen from clover and wildflowers. As if by power of suggestion, I find myself drawn to the shade as well. The temperature has spiked considerably, and my beard suddenly feels like a fur sweater wrapped around my face.

"It's the Mediterranean weather," Casey explains. "Good for almonds, bad for beards. There's only a few places in the world that have hot, dry summers, and cold, wet winters, and the Central Valley is one. Almonds will grow in other places—throughout the Mediterranean region, of course—but nearly ninety percent of the world's almonds are grown right here in California."

Did You Know?

Comprising less than 1 percent of the nations' farmland, nearly 10 percent of America's vegetables originate from California's Grand Central Valley. The Mediterranean-like climate allows it to grow more than 450 different crops, a spectrum that ranges from almonds and artichokes to cranberries, kiwis, and olives.

The couple leads me past a vineyard of Bronx grapes—a sweet, delicate table variety they package and sell to Whole Foods—to an orchard of mature almond trees, broad branches covered with velvety spring fruit. Casey seeks out one tree in particular, standing tiptoe to reach a few unpicked nuts overlooked during last October's harvest. Smiling slyly, she hands me a small brown almond, studying my reaction as I taste it. The flavor is unmistakably amaretto, sending me back a decade to winter meals with my Italian in-laws, where the bittersweet liqueur was sipped from shot glasses after radicchio salad and pasta Bolognese. This particular variety is used for baking, Casey explains, and is one of many different varieties of almonds grown on the farm.

"I grew up with almonds," John recalls, pronouncing the word "ammins." "My dad had eighty acres of trees, and I learned a lot from him, especially about having a strong work ethic. I was a 4-H and FFA kid, so when I graduated college in 1978, I went into farming myself. But I started out with wine grapes. I farmed grapes for fifteen years—for white wine—but the market was just terrible in the eighties, and I couldn't make a go of it. Then, in the early nineties, I switched things up, trying my hand at berries, and that's when I got involved selling at farmers' markets. It's also when I met Casey," he adds, smiling sheepishly. "She was selling her jams right across from my stand."

John rented an almond orchard from his uncle and began attending the Ferry Plaza farmers' market each weekend in San Francisco. A conventional farmer for most of his life, it was feedback from customers that influenced his thinking, gradually nudging him to convert to organic practices.

The biggest difference between the two production methods, John explains, involves nitrogen. Mainstream growers apply three hundred units of nitrogen—via ammonia, derived from fossil fuels—each year. With organics, that's nearly impossible to supply naturally, and the difference shows up in

John's Farm Humor

"You know why we call them 'ammins'? Because you have to shake the L out of them!"

yield. Conventional almond farmers have no trouble reaping two thousand pounds of nuts per acre, whereas organic production harvests roughly half of that. Even with the decreased yields, however, the farmer has never regretted his decision.

"It can be frustrating, though, reading the trade magazines. Everything's so pro-chemical, pro-fertilizer. The way we were taught in agriculture school, there's this implicit threat of Malthusian catastrophe—you know, the theory that population will someday outstrip food supply, and everyone will starve." John regards me thoughtfully behind black-rimmed glasses. "I think people forget our hunger problems come more from wars and social ills than a lack of sprays and fertilizers."

An aversion to synthetic chemicals doesn't make John turn his back to technology. Each fall, he rents a machine called the "shaker," a giant lobster-claw-on-wheels that physically grapples each trunk, vibrating the branches with the intensity of a Labrador slinging water from its coat. The nuts cascade from the trees in a shower of hulls and leaves, then are gathered into wagons via what Casey describes as "a giant vacuum cleaner." After harvest, the almonds are trucked to the huller-sheller, a specialty service that removes the outer shells—typically ending up as cattle feed—and returns the nuts back to the farm. For an organic operation like Lagier Ranches, the almonds are then frozen for several weeks, to kill any worms or insects that might have snuck through the process.

"Next comes the sorting," Casey continues. "We pick through every almond, removing the ones without a perfect outer skin. That thin brown shell you see on each nut?" she says, holding forth a handful of almonds. "You want to discard the chipped and broken ones right away. That's their protective coating; it helps hold in the oil. The

broken ones get made into almond butter, before they lose their moisture."

In the center of the farm is a modest steel warehouse, with bay doors sized to accommodate large trucks. "We built this packing shed fifteen years ago, in order to be diversified," Casey reveals, opening a receiving door and allowing us to step inside. "Not only do we pack our own fruit here, but we've got a commercial kitchen where we make almond butter, jams and jellies, all sorts of things. Plus, we roast and salt almonds for ourselves and others. Susie just finished a batch. Come have a taste."

All I have to do is follow my nose. The smell of hot roasted almonds carries the olfactory magic of freshly baked bread, transforming the utilitarian, tinny warehouse into something homey, something wholesome. Susie uses oversize oven mitts to remove the nuts, which crackle as they cool on silver baking sheets, emitting a soft white-noise like the crumpling of parchment. After a minute they've cooled enough to toss hand to hand. I pop one in my mouth; it's warm and buttery and

sweetly crunchy. No honey glazing, no wasabi infusions, no barbecue flavoring needed. Just pure almonds, roasting on an indirect fire. Bing Crosby left us all a little poorer, having never composed a summer ode to roasted nuts.

Surprisingly, it's green almonds that have become all the rage as of late. Served chilled over ice, lightly dipped into a ramekin of sea salt, the nuts are harvested while still green and eaten raw, shell and all.

"Just like the trees themselves, it goes back to the Mediterranean cultures," Casey explains, as we return to the almond grove. "Palestinians, Lebanese, Syrians, Israelis . . . San Francisco is a very international town, and these are the folks who started requesting green almonds at market. It's what they eat in their home country." She laughs. "So now, other customers start noticing at market, asking, 'Can you really eat them like that?' Yeah," she says, snapping a green almond from the tree, "you can eat them like that! And they're delicious."

She hands me a sage-colored almond, lightly fuzzy and the size of a large peach pit. "Go ahead," she encourages, sensing my reluctance. "Eat the whole thing. They're just perfect right now."

I take a tentative taste, teeth sinking through the firm outer hull, biting it in two. The texture is akin to a watermelon rind, crisp and lightly tart on the tongue, a balancing act of mellow sweetness and satisfying crunch. Halved, the nut reminds me of a geode, strata of bright colors blending into a creamy matrix, with a translucent jelly-like core. This, of course, is the nut itself, a snapshot in time where the almond has formed but not yet hardened. In fact, Casey reveals, the season for green almonds only lasts a few weeks each year, making them difficult to find unless you happen to live nearby.

She snacks on an almond of her own, a thoughtful look on her face. "You know," she continues at last, "we're both cancer survivors, John and me. In fact, John's first wife passed away from leukemia. So going organic, for us at least, it was kind of a no-brainer."

Casey lingers in a cool, shaded row, beneath branches laden with mint-green almonds. "I mean, come on," she adds, gesturing skyward. "Between the weather, the harvests, all the equipment breakdowns . . . we can't control everything. But at least we don't expose ourselves to toxic chemicals anymore, or have them in our food."

A zephyr stirs, and Casey regards the gently swaying boughs. "There's an old saying around here. 'You plant almonds for your kids, and pistachios for your grandkids.' Planting nut trees requires long-term vision, and not everybody thinks like that."

The wind pushes through her hair, scattering loose strands across her cheeks. "I hope these trees are here long after I'm gone. In the meantime, though, this is our IRA, our retirement account. It might only be eighty acres, you know?" She turns, trailing her fingertips along the edge of the leaves. "But for John and me, this is our life. We feel like we're making a difference the best way we know how."

Did You Know?

Botanically classified as a stone fruit instead of a nut, almonds are closely related to peaches and plums. The "nut" is actually the edible seed of the almond fruit.

ALMOND MILK

From Heritage Hollow Farms

Inspired by Lagier Ranches

Makes about 3 cups almond milk

1 cup raw almonds

3 cups water + extra for soaking the almonds

Honey and/or vanilla extract to taste

1. Place the almonds in a bowl, cover with water, and soak overnight. The next day, remove the soaked, plumped almonds from the bowl. Rinse the nuts and make sure they're soft by pinching some of the almonds. Soak them for another few hours if they're not yet soft.

2. Place the almonds in a blender or food processor with the 3 cups of water and blend on high for 2 to 3 minutes, until smooth.

3. Lay some cheesecloth or a fine mesh strainer over a large bowl and place the almond pulp inside. Strain as much of the milk as you can into the bowl.*

4. Sweeten with honey and/or vanilla. Transfer to a 1-quart container with a lid and refrigerate. The almond milk will keep for up to 2 days in the refrigerator.

*You can dry the leftover almond meal and use in recipes that call for almond flour.

PICKLED CHERRIES

From Lagier Ranches

Makes about 1 pint

FARMER'S NOTE: *These are absolutely fabulous with pâté, cheese, or duck. I have also been known to add them as a garnish to vanilla ice cream. The brine is wonderful, and once the cherries are gone, it can be reduced to a syrup and drizzled over just about anything you can think of—it would even work great mixed with sparkling water to create a shrub. I never stem or pit the cherries in this recipe since I prefer them whole, so I like to choose particularly beautiful-looking fruit. Make sure to let people know that the cherries aren't pitted, though, before they eat it. Note that you'll need canning jars and a hot water bath to make this (see page 295 for more on canning). The recipe can be easily increased or decreased depending upon how many cherries you have.*

½ cup dry red wine
½ cup balsamic vinegar
½ cup water
6 tablespoons sugar + extra as necessary
1 bay leaf
6 allspice berries
1 fresh thyme sprig
1 pound cherries, unpitted

1. Combine all the ingredients except the cherries and thyme in a medium saucepan and simmer over medium heat for about 5 minutes. Taste and add additional sugar if necessary. Let cool slightly.

2. Add the thyme sprig to a sterile 1-pint canning jar and fill with the cherries. Pour in the liquid mixture, making sure to get rid of all the air bubbles.

3. Seal the jar and process in a hot water bath for 15 minutes. Allow to sit a few days before using to allow them to pickle. Refrigerate after opening.

CHERRY CLAFOUTIS

From Lagier Ranches

Makes one 10-inch clafoutis

5 tablespoons unsalted butter, melted + a little extra melted butter for the dish

¾ cup sugar

1¼ cups almond flour

⅔ cup unbleached all-purpose flour

Pinch of salt

2 large eggs

⅔ cup milk

1½ pounds cherries, stemmed but not pitted

FARMER'S NOTE: *This is my favorite version of a clafoutis (a custard-like French dessert), although it can be made with any fruit. I always leave the pits in the cherries—best to warn people before—as I think it adds flavor. I make the almond flour from our bitter almonds since I like the strong almond flavor, although some people don't. Sweet almonds or store-bought almond flour (sometimes called almond meal) also work very well.*

1. Preheat the oven to 400°F.

2. Coat the bottom and sides of a round 10-inch baking dish with some of the melted butter. Toss a bit of the sugar into the dish, turning and shaking the dish to cover the inside with a coating of sugar.

3. Pour the remaining sugar into a large bowl and add the almond flour, all-purpose flour, and salt; whisk to blend. Beat the eggs in a separate bowl, then mix in the milk and the remaining melted butter. Add the liquid mixture to the dry ingredients and combine thoroughly.

4. Line the bottom of the prepared baking dish with the cherries. Pour the batter evenly over the fruit. Bake until cooked through, when a knife inserted into the center comes out clean, about 40 minutes. Serve warm or cold.

7

HAYSTACK MOUNTAIN GOAT DAIRY

Goat cheese

The prison guard leans into my driver's side window, asking me to surrender my cell phone, electronics, and any weapons I might have brought with me.

"Weapons?" I repeat, making sure I understand him correctly.

"Pocket knives, switchblades, firearms," he elaborates, speaking in a practiced monotone typically used by middle school gym teachers. My mind flashes back to 1985, when my sister bought me a novelty switchblade comb for my eleventh birthday, styling my hair into a slick Bruce Springsteen coif.

"No, sir," I reply, handing over my cell phone and backpack. To my good fortune, I had parted ways with the comb some twenty-five years earlier. "No weapons."

He nods, satisfied there's no contraband stashed in the recesses of my rented Yaris. "Just follow that guide truck ahead of you, and he'll take you where you need to go." The officer is almost back to the guardhouse when he stops and turns.

"Oh. And, Mr. Pritchard?"

I pump the brakes. "Yes, sir?"

He smiles beneath an immaculately trimmed gold mustache. "Enjoy the goats."

It's surreal to be inside Colorado's Skyline Correctional Center, about two hours southwest of Denver, visiting the largest flock of goats in the state, which provide the milk that will later be trucked to Haystack Mountain Dairy to make cheese. This is my first time inside a prison, and as I follow the pilot truck I take in the view. On my left, narrow-windowed concrete buildings are encircled by looping coils of razor wire, sunlight glinting from polished steel barbs. On my right, however, is why I'm here: to witness farming as a positive correctional philosophy. I pass a vineyard, then a barnyard filled with bighorn sheep. Next, acres of cornstalks have been plowed into the dark soil, the remnants of a successful harvest, all beneath a late November sky spread expansively blue and cloudless.

Agriculture is a cornerstone of Skyline's program, which teaches inmates the basics of crop production and animal husbandry, developing marketable skills that might someday be useful in the outside world. Work on the farms is reserved for minimum-security prisoners who have consistently demonstrated good behavior. Providing fresh air and exercise, as well as hourly pay and bonuses for meeting cleanliness and production benchmarks, placement in the dairy is strictly voluntary yet highly sought-after. Presently, the waiting list is nearly a thousand long.

Today, I've come to visit the dairy, and the scenery doesn't disappoint. In the near distance, the front range of the Rocky Mountains rises jagged and untamed, the Arkansas River a glinting, silvery ribbon at its feet. The guide truck swings a sharp right and the austere prison buildings fall away behind us, replaced with open cropland. Driving toward the river, we

Did You Know?

Globally, goats are one of our oldest domesticated species, dating back more than 9,000 years. Although there are 450 million goats worldwide—spanning more than 200 different breeds—only 7 percent are represented within the United States.

navigate a winding road of crushed pink rock. Ferrous bluffs of sandstone loom two hundred feet above our heads, while scrubby junipers and ponderosa pines flank the road, sprouting between boulders that tumbled down from the heights. It's a scene straight out of the Old West, an exquisite Louis L'Amour landscape. All that's really missing, I tell myself as the pilot truck rounds a bend, is two or three shaggy frontier goats, and the canvas would be complete.

Two or three . . . or, as it turns out, fifteen hundred.

"Yeah," says Mary Provost, head of operations and goat-herder-in-chief. "And next year we're holding back some young does, stock we'd ordinarily sell to local farmers. If all goes well, we're planning to expand to seventeen hundred. But there's always been more demand for our milk than we can produce, so we've got to grow sensibly."

Stretched along a feed bunker, a line of milk goats are contentedly munching sprigs of mint-green alfalfa. Nubians, Saanens, Toggenburgs, La Manchas—all the major dairy breeds are represented, a mottled palette of browns and taupes and dusty whites, wispy beards hanging from softly rounded chins. An Alpine—Mary's favorite breed—cocks its head and regards me with long, rectangular pupils, seeming to request a good scratching. I happily oblige, reaching over the fence to rub behind its floppy ears. The goat closes its eyes, lips sloped in the faintest hint of smile, thoroughly savoring the moment.

The goat pens—perhaps more appropriately described as spacious loafing areas—are easily more than a thousand feet square. These are home to about two hundred does apiece, providing ample room for the animals to comfortably spread out, sunning themselves in the gentle autumn sunshine. Long, airy shelters are deep-bedded with yellow

straw, and a large, mounded hill of earth and stone rises from the middle of each yard—a miniature mountain for climbing and frolic. Goats are famous climbers, and accordingly there are about a dozen does scattered across the mound, with a lone goat perched at the peak like a mountaineer surveying new territory. Most remarkably, with so many goats and so many pens, there's not the faintest trace of urine or manure odors.

Mary nods. "We run a tight ship here. The pens are thoroughly cleaned each week, and the manure ends up back on the crop fields for fertilizer." She gestures to an inmate driving past on a tractor, a box spreader dragging a smooth trail through the Colorado dust. "Everyone's got a specific job, a firm routine. With thirty-two workers, that's the way it has to be."

She leads me to the dairy parlor, greeting inmates and goats alike along the way. A sturdy, fit woman in her mid-fifties, Mary has worked around goats her entire life. When a friend mentioned that Skyline was seeking a dairy manager to take over their fledgling goat program, Mary, a grandmother of five, decided to apply. "I was just more curious than anything," she admits. "I wanted to see firsthand what a prison knew about raising goats. Turns out," she adds wryly, "they didn't know much. I've spent the last nine years here, building infrastructure, putting in frost-free waterers, making this a year-round system so we'll always have plenty of milk. Isn't that right, Mr. Martinez?"

"Yes, ma'am," replies a wiry, bearded man in his mid-thirties. Wearing prison fatigues and a blaze-orange safety smock, Martinez supervises operations within the dairy barn. The workday begins at four in the morning, and the third, final shift doesn't end until well past nine in the evening. Twice daily, he explains, the goats are led into the two-sided parlor and milked twenty per row for a few minutes each. Working fifteen hundred goats takes about four hours in the morning, and then it starts all over again at two in the afternoon. Between shifts, the room is washed and scrubbed clean; it's now eleven

o'clock, and two men with hoses and brushes are sanitizing the concrete where the goats were recently milked.

Back outside, the farm is bathed in golden autumn light. "You've got to understand," Mary volunteers kindly, "most of these boys have never worked a steady job, or even know what it's like to get a paycheck. They've come straight off the streets, and things like work schedules, routines . . . these are new concepts for most of them." As we talk, two men approach us with pitchforks slung over their shoulders.

Her gentle tone becomes suddenly stentorian. "And where are we headed today, Mr. Timmons?"

Built like an offensive lineman, with a rounded paunch and forearms sheathed in flame tattoos, Mr. Timmons doesn't hesitate. "To the kidding barn, ma'am. Gonna feed the babies straw."

Mary sighs deeply, folds her arms, and addresses his companion.

"Mr. Watts? You've got seniority here. Would you please correct Mr. Timmons?"

Mr. Watts is a handsome man in his mid-twenties, and his tone is empathetic as he sets his partner straight. "We feed the goats hay, right? Not straw. The straw's just for bedding." Noting his partner's confusion, he continues. "Don't worry, man. When I first got here, I made the same mistake. Come on, I'll show you."

Mary watches them go, lips pursed with grandmotherly exasperation. "I always match a more experienced worker to a newbie," she explains, once they're out of earshot. "That way there's mentoring and accountability. Mr. Watts, he's a good one. Been with me for nine months."

I watch the pair disappear into the shadow of the barn and observe Mr. Watts gesturing to a stack of alfalfa bales. "So when they get out," I ask, "will any of these guys work at dairies?"

Mary considers the question. "A few of them do. Sure. But let's be honest. With fewer and fewer farms these days, do you imagine hundreds of dairy jobs out there waiting to be filled?

"No," she replies, answering her own question. "More than anything else, these boys are learning a work ethic. Afterwards, when I hear about someone finding a job and sticking with it, that's when I'm satisfied. That's my measure of success."

Of course, on a dairy, success must be also measured in milk. This is a fact that doesn't go unappreciated by Haystack Mountain, the primary recipient of Skyline's daily milkings.

John Scaggs, Haystack's coordinator of farmers' markets and cheese distribution, leads me past a gleaming tank where the milk is received. "Simply put," he says, patting the stainless steel, "if it wasn't for Skyline, we wouldn't have enough milk to meet customer demand."

It's a special partnership for sure. Founded near Longmont, Colorado, in 1988, Haystack was started by former school administrator Jim Schott, who had dreamed of homesteading along the rugged Colorado range. Setting out with four does and a buck, he slowly grew his flock, selling fresh goat cheese and milk shares to local customers, and attending farmers' markets in the Boulder area. Business was slow at first. In the late eighties, local, artisanal goat cheese was nearly unheard of, with most product shipped in from France and the remainder trickling in from California.

As word spread through farmers' markets about Jim's wonderful goat cheese, however, it wasn't long before restaurants began inquiring. By the early nineties, the farmer expanded his dairy to 125 head, the maximum that was allowed in the county. But when major grocery stores—first Wild Oats, followed by Alfalfa's, Kroger, and Whole Foods—came calling, these new accounts quickly outstripped supply. As a solution, he reached out to nearby goat dairies, hoping collaboration with his fellow farmers would satisfy the rising demand for his cheese.

The strategy worked for several years. But one by one, as the dairymen began to retire, there was no one there to take their place.

"You know what you should do?" one of the farmers told him. "Call down to Skyline, in Cañon City. They've had a cow dairy down there since the early 1900s. Maybe they'd be interested in raising goats."

After several meetings—as well as promises by Haystack to invest in infrastructure and training—a partnership was struck. Fast-forward seven years. Haystack Mountain, located in a small, nondescript warehouse three hours north of Skyline's dairy, takes in an average of forty-five hundred gallons of milk a week. Still, it's barely enough to meet the ever-growing demand for dairy goat products.

"For consumers, it's become a big health issue," John explains. "People have learned that goat's milk is easier to digest than a cow's . . . it has to do with the chemical structure of the fats. Oversimplifying it, smaller animals produce smaller fat molecules. Because we're closer in size to goats than we are cows, our bodies have an easier time breaking down the milk."

Inside the creamery, production is in full swing. The room carries the pleasant twang of fresh goat milk, and a thin glaze of butterfat slickens the concrete floor. Here, the milk is received several times weekly, pasteurized at 145 degrees Fahrenheit, then immediately fermented with the aid of starter cultures. By the next morning, the milk has thickened into curd, which is then poured into white cloth bags and stacked four high; beneath its own weight, it seeps translucent yellow whey into a catch basin.

A day later, the curd goes in one of two directions: (1) into a drying room, curing an additional day before being hand-molded into shape, or (2) straight into a mixing bowl, and lightly whipped with salt. Today, I get to see both.

The paddle spins furiously in the mixing bowl, and a creamy batch of chèvre appears right before my eyes. I'm offered a finger's width, impossibly white and the precise consistency of billowy summer clouds. The flavor is bright and citrusy, offering clean, sweet notes of pine. It reminds me of a perfectly hopped beer—smooth yet robust, leaving the palate craving more. The dairy's most popular variety, John relates that chefs crumble this cheese over salads. But I imagine it spread over fresh sourdough bread, enjoyed while quaffing my favorite pale ale.

On the other side of the room, chief cheese maker Jackie Chang, fifty, is hand-salting miniature pyramids of Roquefort. After moving from Taiwan to America in 1981 at age seventeen, Jackie spent twenty years helping manage her family's restaurant business. Her life was changed, however, when she visited Jim's goat farm as a chaperone for her daughter's Brownie troop.

"It was early spring, and there were baby goats everywhere," Jackie recalls, her face lighting up at the memory. "That was it. I fell in love with the goats right there on the spot."

At the end of the troop's tour she asked if she could come volunteer, and the farmer agreed. Every morning she awoke at three, arriving at four to assist with milking and learn the basics of goat husbandry. After a year, her passion undiminished, Jim asked if she'd like a permanent position making cheese.

Jackie laughs merrily. "Growing up in Taiwan, there was no such thing as cheese. My father, he bought Kraft Singles on the black market. You know, one slice at a time. So I asked myself, 'What do I know about making cheese?' Not a lot. But I read, studied online, paid attention. Now, eleven years later, I make over twenty different varieties."

Award-winning varieties, it should be noted. Last year, Jackie propelled Haystack to two national

Jackie's Advice for New Cheese Makers

"If you're really serious, start by scrubbing the floors each day, making sure everything's perfectly clean. It's the little details that are most important. This is how I test new people on my staff. Without great habits, you can't make great cheese."

gold medals in the hard-cheese category and landed first runner-up for their Green Chile Jack. It's through subtle differences in culturing, aging, and rind washing that Jackie creates nearly two dozen types of cheese from a single batch of goat milk. But despite her self-taught success, she's quick to point out that not everything can be learned from a book.

"Making cheese, it's like raising a child," she says earnestly. "When they're cold, you give them a coat. When they're hot, you take the coat off." She opens the door to the aging room, gesturing to a row of obelisk-shaped Roqueforts, powdered gray with poplar ash. "You've got to live with the cheeses, recognize the temperatures, the different smells. They all have different personalities, can't you tell?"

She holds out a creamy wedge of goat cheese, a fist-size work of art sculpted by a master's hands. "Look," she says, "when a cheese is finished, you can see the craftsman in the product. Pretend you're a customer shopping at a grocery store. Everything you need to know about the person who made that cheese, it's right there in front of you."

Did You Know?

Producing blue cheese typically requires a facility unto itself. The molds are nearly impossible to keep contained and, once airborne, can quickly colonize other cheeses.

Jackie dusts it with salt before placing it onto an aging rack. "This is the most honest work in the world. No secrets. The cheese will tell you everything."

No secrets. So easy in principle, so difficult in execution. I think back to the goats, contentedly munching alfalfa hay, and to the men intent on caring for them, passing time as we all must. For a few hours, everything was transparent beneath a perfect Colorado sky.

I've spent a lifetime amending my own behaviors, seeking improvement through the simple toil of farmwork. Searching for answers. We each have our own paths to reconcile; there's no mystery in that. Other secrets, perhaps, should be left to the goats: forever on the lookout for a good scratch, a sunny perch on a mountaintop, and tranquilly viewing the world through their enigmatic, rectangular pupils.

Did You Know?

Cheese tastes best when it's above 50 degrees Fahrenheit; cheese knives create thin slices to help warm the cheese quickly. For optimal flavor, warm cold cheese on your tongue for five seconds before chewing.

MUSHROOM AND CHÈVRE FRITTATA

From Haystack Mountain Goat Dairy

Serves 4 to 6

3 tablespoons olive oil

2 garlic cloves, finely chopped

1 pound mixed mushrooms (cremini, shiitake, oyster, etc.), trimmed as necessary, sliced or chopped

3 fresh thyme sprigs

8 large eggs

1 cup (½ pint) heavy cream or half-and-half

4 ounces (½ cup) crumbled Haystack Mountain Boulder Chèvre, if available in your area, or other soft goat cheese

8 fresh mint leaves, finely chopped

Salt and freshly ground black pepper

1 teaspoon unsalted butter

This delightful recipe was supplied to Haystack from Chef Hugo Matheson of The Kitchen, in Boulder, Colorado.

1. Preheat the oven to 350°F.

2. Heat the oil in a 10-inch, oven-safe, nonstick skillet over medium heat. Add the garlic and cook until the garlic is light brown, about 1 minute. Stir in the mushrooms and thyme. Increase the heat to high and sauté until the mushroom liquid has evaporated, about 10 minutes.

3. Beat the eggs, cream or half-and-half, goat cheese, mint, and a sprinkle of salt and pepper in a bowl. Add the mushroom mixture and combine all the ingredients together. Adjust the seasoning as necessary.

4. Return the now-empty skillet to medium heat and add the butter. Let it sizzle slightly, then add the egg-mushroom mixture. Cook until the bottom is slightly set, then stir. Repeat this process several times (this helps distribute heat throughout the mixture).

5. Place the skillet in the oven and cook the frittata until a knife inserted into the middle comes out clean, about 10 minutes. Remove from the oven and let rest for 10 minutes. Turn the frittata out onto a plate, or serve it straight from the pan.

TIP:

You can also cook these in muffin tins for mini frittatas—they're easy to warm up, turning any leftovers into quick, on-the-go breakfasts or snacks.

ROASTED BEET AND ARUGULA SALAD

WITH CHÈVRE FONDUE AND SHERRY VINAIGRETTE

From Haystack Mountain Goat Dairy

Serves 4 to 6

3 pounds medium beets

½ cup olive oil

Salt and freshly cracked white pepper

Chèvre Fondue (recipe follows)

Sherry Vinaigrette (recipe follows)

1 pound arugula

3 to 4 tablespoons local honey

This delicious and boldly flavorful salad came to Haystack from Chef Matt Christianson, of Q's Restaurant at the Hotel Boulderado in Boulder, Colorado.

1. Preheat the oven to 350°F.

2. Place the beets in a large bowl, then add the oil and sprinkle with salt and pepper. Toss to coat the beets. Transfer the beets to a large, deep baking dish and cover with aluminum foil. Roast until the beets feel tender when pierced with a small knife, about 2 hours.

3. While the beets are roasting, prepare the Sherry Vinaigrette and Chèvre Fondue from the recipes that follow.

4. Let the roasted beets cool slightly; when cool enough to handle, remove the skins and dice the beets into ¼-inch cubes.* Set aside.

5. Toss the arugula lightly in some of the vinaigrette, then plate it on a serving dish. Toss the diced beets in some vinaigrette as well—if desired, you can use a ring mold to form the beets into an attractive shape. Lay the beets on top of the arugula. Drizzle the Chèvre Fondue and honey around the plate. Enjoy!

*Use a paper towel to peel the skins off the beets; the friction of the towel helps them peel faster. Also, consider wearing gloves if you don't want the juice to stain your hands.

CHÈVRE FONDUE

Pour the cream into a medium heavy-bottomed saucepan and simmer over low heat until reduced by half, about 2 minutes, watching closely so it doesn't burn. Add the goat cheese, whisking until melted. Season with salt and pepper to taste. Keep in a warm place until needed.

½ cup heavy cream

8 ounces Haystack Mountain Chèvre, if available in your area, or other soft goat cheese

Salt and freshly ground black pepper

SHERRY VINAIGRETTE

Whisk the vinegar, shallot, mustard, and honey together in a medium bowl. Add salt and pepper to taste, and whisk to incorporate. Slowly whisk in the oil. Season with additional salt, pepper, oil, and vinegar as needed.

½ cup sherry vinegar + extra as needed

2 tablespoons minced shallot

1 teaspoon Dijon mustard

1 teaspoon local honey

Sea salt

Freshly ground black pepper

Freshly ground white pepper

1¼ cups olive oil

8

MATT ROMERO FARMS

DIXON, NEW MEXICO

Vegetables and chile peppers

////////////////////////////////

There's no denying it. Matt Romero's corner of New Mexico is green, absolutely lush with vegetation. "What were you imagining?" the farmer chides good-naturedly. "Nothing but tumbleweeds and sand down here?"

An hour's drive north of Santa Fe, I certainly had my doubts. The drive was spectacularly scenic, with crumbling, chalky outcroppings flanking sepia hills of sandy gravel. Juniper and sage dotted the austere foothills, a glimpse of green from the corner of my eye. Georgia O'Keeffe cultivated her genius here, transfiguring the exquisite symmetry of sand and sky, the sunshine brightening the braided arroyos. But aside from occasional fleurettes of alfalfa swaying near the pavement's edge, I hadn't seen anything to foreshadow the verdant agricultural landscape I was now witnessing. A tall, broad-shouldered man, Matt drops to one knee, cupping a handful of rich fluvial sediments.

"People think of New Mexico as being dry, and some parts certainly are. But we can grow almost anything here, as long as we have the water. This soil is *alive*."

The Rio Grande, lined with locust and cottonwood, rolls volubly past the farm, just a short distance from the production fields. The water is swift and cold, charged with mountain snowmelt after an especially bracing winter.

Matt stoops over a length of black drip tape, a tentacled network of hoses that slowly saturate the soil.

"Hey, watch this." He twists a small red valve and water jets ten feet into the air, arcing gracefully over newly planted broccoli. "The Rio Grande never runs dry, even in the hottest summers." Matt shuts off the valve, surveying his fields. "There's so much opportunity to grow food here. All we need is more locals interested in farming."

At the end of a long row of freshly plowed earth, assistant Adolpho is planting potatoes: Yukon Golds, Purple Peruvians, Red Thumbs, French White La Rattes. With climate change, Matt explains, the frosts in this region keep getting later each season. Ever adapting, he plants vegetable varieties that better withstand the cold. "We're putting in the first onions this morning." He ticks the names off on his fingertips. "Garlic, celery, carrots, and cauliflower. A frost might wilt a couple leaves, but it doesn't knock them out."

Matt Romero, fifty-five, farms eleven acres of vegetables with two full-time employees, on land his grandfather purchased nearly a century ago. Growing up in the neighborhood as a child, he recalls widespread poverty with few prospects beyond work at the casino or at nearby Los Alamos, the nuclear-research facility where the atomic bomb was invented. By the age of seventeen, he was more than ready to leave. He worked his way into the restaurant business, eventually becoming an executive chef, opening high-profile concept restaurants in Denver, Colorado. As time passed, however, something began to change.

"The first couple of years it was fun, exciting. But one morning as I was driving into Denver, I looked up at that city

Did You Know?

Carrots were originally purple, and were first cultivated in Afghanistan. The Dutch cultivated the widely recognized orange variety starting in the seventeenth century.

skyline and said to myself, 'Oh no. Not again.' I just didn't want to do it anymore, that endless grind." He pauses to thin a cluster of beet greens, dusting his hands before continuing. "When you're a manager, it means you're on call twenty-four hours a day. If someone doesn't show, guess what? *You* show. And that's a lot of pressure."

Along the rusted perimeter fence, spring carrots sprout ornately alongside our footpath. "Suddenly," Matt continues, "it occurred to me: Instead of working my way up the ladder, maybe it was time to work my way 'down.' All the way down . . . to the soil, you know? To the food. So I made up my mind. I decided to come back home, and take over the family farm."

He exhales a deep sigh. "The first few years were *brutal*. I didn't know how to farm, how to garden. Those early months, I almost killed myself with work. Coming back as a chef, I weighed over three hundred pounds, and I lost ninety my first year. Ninety pounds!" He pats his stomach. "Turns out, farming was harder than any restaurant opening. But it also taught me: I'm capable of doing a lot more than I thought I was."

His uncle, who had been managing the farm for years, stepped into a mentorship role, generously sharing his knowledge. But Matt soon discovered that years of conventional

Matt's Chef Advice

"I tell people: Bring me any food in the world. If I can't cook it with olive oil and salt, it can't be cooked! Whatever else you put into a recipe, it's just extra."

practices had taken their toll on his family's land; the pesticides and commercial fertilizers had reached a tipping point. Chemicals that had reliably worked for his uncle were suddenly less effective and were burning the crops, due to saturation in the soil.

"I'd see diseases right after I planted the seedlings," Matt recalls. "Anyone could tell the conventional way wasn't working. Then, about ten years ago, I met this organic farmer and asked him for a tour of his farm. It changed my whole life. He showed me how to set up my rows, install drip tape, how to use compost. That's when things really turned around. A few years later I was actually profitable, and able to buy more land."

It's early May, and parts of the farm are still blanketed in cover crops: oats, wheat, and field peas. The vegetation serves to protect otherwise bare ground throughout the winter, stabilizing soil carbon and preventing erosion, before being plowed into the earth as fertilizer come springtime.

"This is how our soil stays healthy year-round," Matt reveals. "Most people think you've got to buy bags of fertilizer, nitrogen, things like that. No," he says emphatically. "With natural farming, it's more about bacterial health. When you leave soil bare all winter, the beneficial bacteria dies. There's no place for it to live. It needs root systems, moisture, fungus to feed on.

"A lot of farmers, they leave their soils barren all winter and end up saying, 'Huh. I wonder why my crops didn't do as well as last year?' But when we're done harvesting in the fall," he continues, beaming, "the cover is so thick, it looks like we've been growing a lawn instead of a fallow field all winter."

He picks at a few weeds, discarding them along the path. "You know, if it wasn't for weeds, I think everyone would be farming. Which is why they make Roundup," he adds jokingly, eyebrows arched above his sunglasses. "That's how you get rid of weeds, right? Without working." Matt smiles ironically. "Of course we'd never use that stuff. But we also have to charge more, because of the extra labor."

The farmer stops in his tracks. "Some people say food like this is expensive. 'Expensive' only means you bought something you don't like. My customers want to know, 'Is it tasty? Will I like it? How was it raised?' If you're happy with what you're getting, then that's not expensive. It's a value."

Ten years ago, Matt recognized an opportunity when the Santa Fe Farmers' Market decided to remain open year-round. He modified his production, moving to equal parts seasonal produce and durable root-cellar-type offerings. Last winter, he sold fifteen thousand pounds of potatoes and two thousand pounds of garlic, along with cabbages, kohlrabi, and his specialty: flamboyantly hot chile peppers.

"Adapting to what the market wants, that's a big component of success. I can't grow the same things my ancestors grew and expect to sell out at farmers' markets." A ripple of emotion plays across his face. "Look, I'm a *norteño*. Translated, that means

Did You Know?

"Roots are the only part of the plant that need oxygen," Matt explains. "That's why some farmers till the soil, to break up the compaction and make sure the air can find its way beneath the ground. If we can keep enough air in the soil, the water can percolate through without displacing the oxygen. Water them too much? The roots can't get air, and the plant drowns."

Northern Mexico Hispanic." He spreads his arms, taking in the view. "This was all Mexico for a long time, right? And the people living here, they were Mexicans. There's a running joke around here: 'We're conquistadors! No, we're not!' You have to know our history to understand the joke, the dual nature. It means we're half-Spanish, and half-native."

When Juan de Oñate arrived in the late 1500s as a viceroy to King Philip II, Matt recounts, he was charged with settling the Southwest. "He picked this place because agriculture was already established; the native people had been farming here for generations. In those days, the hardest thing was food. You either grew it, killed it, or stole it. Guess which one the Spanish chose?" He laughs sardonically. "Even though we're half-Spanish, and it's been over four hundred years, Oñate's still not too popular around here."

We navigate a wooden staircase, pausing on a small bridge. Beneath us, clear water gurgles through an earthen sluice, several feet wide and deep. "This *açequia*—'water ditch' in English—was made hundreds of years ago by the natives. It's six miles long, all constructed by hand, and we still use it to this day." He studies the water, considering. "You've got to realize, my ancestors were the poorest of the poor in this country. But as long as they had water, they always had food. It's how they survived."

The farmer opens the doors to his greenhouse, and a steamy breath of humidity exhales from the cavernous building. Plywood tables are laden with seedlings: tomatoes and eggplants, basil and arugula. Matt pulls a pepper from its pot, studying a tangle of white roots, then replaces it. "Healthy," he says. "Healthy . . . and *hot*."

Love them or fear them, everyone has an opinion about chile peppers. On the drive from Santa Fe,

I had noticed politicians' substituting J's with J-shaped peppers on campaign posters; beyond a doubt, the chile is fundamental to New Mexico's identity. Naturally, Romero doesn't disappoint with his varieties.

"Poblanos, Japanese shishitos, padrons. Some are sweet, some hot. Some are for tapas, some for roasting. Look over here," he says, striding past the curing shed, where peppers, strung like vermillion question marks, are drying in long rows. "I want to show you an heirloom, a variety my uncle raised thirty years before I started farming."

The farmer opens a pillow-size bag, stuffed to capacity with papery, desiccated peppers. The chiles are a deep, smoldering red, the intense smoky hue of scorched firebrick.

"These are Alcalde Improved," he says, holding out a finger-size specimen. A fruity aroma of dried cherry and damson

Did You Know?

A green chile is an immature pepper, harvested before it turns red.

plum wafts from the bag, mixed with something more sultry, more mysterious. "They're loaded with capsaicin," Matt continues, tearing off a tiny piece. "Here. Eat this molecule."

I love hot food, and within seconds the tiny flake of chile gives me all the flavor—and heat—I can handle. The burn starts on the tip of my tongue before spreading along my cheeks, flaming straight to the roof of my mouth. The sensation is momentarily intense but finishes sweetly, delivering the stone fruit flavors of cherry and plum I first detected. Matt studies me attentively, like a firefighter waiting with an extinguisher. When the heat has passed I give him two thumbs up, and he smiles approvingly.

"The thing to do is take fresh peppers like this from the market and toast them in your oven for three minutes. Then, throw them in a blender with a little water, and really grind them. I'm talking, go get yourself a cup of coffee, walk around the block . . . leave it mixing for seven, eight minutes. Then, just pour them in a skillet, add a little salt, and simmer. Simple. That's how you make a traditional chili."

The Southwestern morning has slipped away, and Matt pauses, leaning against the doorjamb of the greenhouse. Behind him, a sea of purple-headed chive sways dreamily, drowsing in the midday sunshine.

"People ask me, 'What would you do differently if you had to start over?' You know, I don't think I'd change much. I'd start small, just like I had to. Then, I'd produce as much as my knowledge allowed, only expanding after I gained experience. I didn't buy my first tractor for six years, until I actually knew what I needed. If more people did that, I think you'd see a lot of successful farms in this country."

Did You Know?

The world's hottest chile pepper is called the Carolina Reaper, a golf-ball-size dynamo four hundred times hotter than a jalapeño. Dairy products, rich in casein, are a natural antidote to a pepper's heat-inducing capsaicin.

EGGPLANT SANDWICH

From Matt Romero Farms

Serves 1

FARMER'S NOTE: *Our favorite eggplant for this sandwich is the Barbarella. Our favorite tomato? The Cherokee Purple, an heirloom variety.*

½ cup unbleached all-purpose flour

1 teaspoon dried basil

1 teaspoon paprika

1 large egg

2 tablespoons milk

1 cup panko (Japanese bread crumbs)

Two ½-inch-thick slices large Italian eggplant (the size of a slice of bread), peeled

Olive oil

1 ounce local soft goat cheese

2 thin slices heirloom tomato

1 large poblano chile, roasted, peeled, and seeded

4 fresh basil, or 6 to 8 fresh spinach or arugula leaves

2 slices red onion

Coarse salt

1. Combine the flour, basil, and paprika in a shallow bowl. Whisk the egg and milk together in a second shallow bowl. Place the panko in a third shallow bowl. Toss the eggplant slices one at a time in the seasoned flour until well coated; next, place them in the egg wash; then dredge them in the panko until well coated.

2. Heat a small amount of oil in a medium nonstick skillet over medium-high heat. When the oil starts to shimmer, throw some panko into the oil; if it turns golden brown, the oil is hot enough (it should be about 350°F if you want to test it with a thermometer). Fry the eggplant on both sides until crispy and golden brown. Drain the eggplant briefly on paper towels.

3. Place one eggplant slice on a plate and spread the goat cheese evenly over the top., Add the tomato, poblano, basil, and onion, season with salt, and top with the remaining eggplant slice. Skewer the sandwich with two toothpicks, one on each side, and cut the sandwich on the diagonal to expose the beautiful layers.

RED CHILI CON CARNE

From Matt Romero Farms

Serves 3 or 4

2 ounces Romero Farms red chile pods, if available in your area, or other red chile pods, stemmed and seeded

4 cups water + extra as needed

1 pound ground meat (beef, pork, turkey, elk, or buffalo)

¼ cup unbleached all-purpose flour

1 tablespoon chopped garlic

2 teaspoons kosher salt

This rich, hearty chili pairs wonderfully with freshly made beans and tortillas.

1. Place the chiles in a large saucepan and cover them with water. Cover the pot and bring to a boil; boil for 20 minutes. Remove from the heat and let the chiles soak for 10 minutes. Drain the chiles, reserving the cooking liquid, and place them in a blender with 2 cups of the cooking liquid, adding up to 3 cups if necessary. (Caution: Do not overfill the blender.) Puree at the highest speed until smooth, 4 to 5 minutes.

2. Brown the ground meat in a heavy-bottomed 6-quart Dutch oven over medium heat. Add the flour, garlic, and salt and cook for 5 minutes. Add the pureed chiles and 4 cups water. Simmer for 15 minutes, adding additional water if necessary to thin the chili to your desired consistency. Serve with your favorite accompaniments.

9

BLACK OAK HOLLER FARM

FRAZIERS BOTTOM, WEST VIRGINIA

Acorn-finished hogs

///////////////////////////////////

Chuck Talbott speaks pig.

"Whoo-oop! Whoooo-oop!" The farmer cradles a hand against his cheek, his voice echoing across a misty West Virginia meadow. The sound is a cross between battle cry and invitation, a melodious call to arms—or in this case, a call to hams.

In unison, forty barrel-shaped durocs raise their heads, abandoning a morning of glorious, muddy rooting to heed the clarion. Bounding and snorting, just short of a stampede, they gallop into a fresh pasture of millet, their rust-colored backs disappearing beneath the waving green forage. Moments later they've vanished entirely, abandoned in breakfast.

"One of the best parts of my job." Chuck, sixty-five, smiles through a gray, grizzled beard. He gestures toward the field of grain, belt-buckle-high and thick as the bristles on a razorback. "A few months ago, that was a rooted-up paddock, just like the one they came off today. Now we'll broadcast seed behind them, maybe barley, maybe pumpkins. It's all fodder for the hogs, an experiment to see what will grow best."

My mind wanders, and I imagine pigs in a pumpkin patch, munching their way into gourds that accidentally become stuck on their heads. Jack-o'-lanterned hogs squealing blindly through the pasture? That would be a Halloween shindig of epic proportions.

Did You Know?

Oaks don't produce acorns every year. Instead, the trees operate on mysterious production cycles, where bumper crops might fall for three years, then yield no nuts at all the following season.

Chuck, on the other hand, is all business. He strides across the field, reconnecting the electric polywire through which the hogs have just passed. It rained hard the night before, and the paddock looks like hand-mixed brownie dough—lumpy, moist, and rich. More accurately, I realize, the soil resembles a freshly tilled garden, its cover crop of field peas harvested and the residue turned beneath the ground as fertilizer. Forty sturdy snouts, it seems, can do the work of one man with a plow. While some farmers might bicker over the efficiency of free-ranging pigs, I'd argue that you can't eat a tractor. Besides, where's the fun in life without trying new things?

Experimentation, in fact, is part of the mission at Black Oak Holler. Just minutes from West Virginia's state capital and a morning's drive to Cincinnati, Pittsburgh, Lexington, or Charlotte, the farm is ideally located to serve metropolitan areas. That is, if pure production was all that mattered. But Chuck began farming with a firm goal: create a sustainable system for raising pigs on the Allegheny Plateau, fattening them—as is traditionally done in Spain—on acorns, walnuts, and hickories, and make it replicable so others could copy his methods. In a region most famously noted for logging and coal mining, he wanted to prove that fragile mountain soils could be restored, even enhanced, through carefully managed livestock. No easy task in this land of rolling hills, where farmers jokingly grumble they occasionally fall straight out of their cornfields.

A former professor at North Carolina A&T State University, the desire to teach seems to come naturally to Talbott. He founded the university's sustainable swine program in 1994, spending the next ten years researching everything from the breeding of piglets to the curing of hams. But the farmer readily admits he'd rather be working the land than grading papers in an office, one of the main reasons he found solace in this isolated corner of the state. "Why would anyone want to wear a suit and tie?" he asks, garbed in a straw hat and suspenders. "I was always meant to be outdoors, to be a farmer."

Standing at the foot of his valley, gazing upward into the rugged mountains, who could blame him? Colloquially known as "hollers," the Appalachians are replete with steep, hidden valleys and wooded canyons bisected by rambling brooks, the moss-slick rocks composing a topographical braille. Hickory and walnut trees punctuate the rocky terrain, with impenetrable thickets of rhododendron and sassafras softening rock breaks of shale and sandstone. Chuck's 270 acres is textbook Appalachia, mountains meeting at precipitous angles, ephemeral springs

trickling water clear as moonshine from the gray, lichened stones.

Once towering as high as the Alps and the Rockies, the Appalachians are among the oldest mountains on earth, now weathered nearly to their roots. The ancient orogeny still echoes through this wild hollow, with a cobbled, single-lane road the solitary access to the valley's head. Chuck seems at home with the wildness, the wilderness. In fact, he's spent a lifetime acclimating himself to the challenges, gaining experience through decades of world travel.

"I grew up in Upstate New York, north of Syracuse. Dairy country. My dad was big into breeding horses, but he passed away when I was twelve. So to make money, all through high school I rented out the stalls and worked on neighboring dairies. Once high school was over, I started traveling."

He spent a season as a ranch hand in Cody, Wyoming, then a summer as a trail guide in Montana. After a few years at Colorado State University, the travel bug bit again. "I always remembered watching those Westerns as a boy, asking, 'Dad, can men still be cowboys?' 'Sure,' he told me. 'In Australia.' I guess I always had that in the back of my mind, being a cowboy in the Outback. So one day I just dropped out of college, and that's where I went."

He pauses, reflecting. "In those days, Americans couldn't get work permits, and I ended up in New Zealand working sheep for a year. Then someone told me, 'Hey, just go to the Outback, tell them you're Canadian. They'll never check.' And he was right. I spent a year and a half in the Northern Territory, near Katherine. But it was too complicated to settle there, so I ended up coming back to the States, getting a master's at Virginia Tech. Then I spent six years in Africa, in Cameroon, helping with their dairy genetics. After I wrapped up my PhD at NC State, I started the sustainable hog program at A&T, and never looked back."

So how does a world traveler end up in the mountains of West Virginia? Evidently, by possessing a farmer's intuition. In 1978, a side trip to visit his sister in nearby Huntington led him to an old tobacco farm, wild and wonderful and with jaw-droppingly cheap acreage compared to anywhere else he'd been. Knowing that he was only passing through, and not even certain about what he'd do with the land, Chuck pulled the trigger and bought himself a farm. It would be twenty-five years before he officially returned.

When he finally did, in 2004, he arrived with a fully con-ceived plan, and the appropriate experience to execute it. "Let me show you my new barn," he beams, gesturing to an open-sided pole building with a concrete floor. "My own design; the only one like it. We'll farrow our sows in here—have piglets, you understand—then when we're ready, turn them loose straight onto pasture without having to transport them."

Hands in pockets, he admires the humble splendor of the building. "Hardly anyone farrows like this, out in the open air. It's modeled after a British farmer named Keith Thornton; he's been doing it successfully for years." A tractor rolls noisily past, hitched to a low-riding wagon that barely clears the ground. "But come on," the farmer says. "We've still got hogs to move. Let me show you the boys."

The boys, it turns out, are two enormous Eurasian wild boars named Bert and Ernie. "A friend called me one day," Chuck recalls, "and said he'd come across a litter of wild piglets—the mother had been killed by a passing car. He asked me if I wanted any of them, so I took the males, and raised them myself."

The farmer nods at the boars, bristle-backed with bright white tusks protruding from their lower lips. Why breed wild boars to domesticated stock? To pass along desirable attributes, the professor explains. Wild genetics add natural vigor that can't be found in commercial hogs, pigs specifically bred to live out their days in concrete feedlots. The concept makes sense; if you're going to successfully breed hogs in a wild holler, I reason, then you'd better stack the genetic deck, placing the odds in your favor.

And that's precisely Chuck's goal: to raise hogs that thrive on the mountain slopes, naturally fattening on acorns. In a state where mining is the primary economic engine, the farmer is banking on a loftier commodity, one that drops straight out of the sky.

"That's the whole goal here," he explains, "matching the hogs to the terrain, like they've done for centuries in Spain. Pigs have an uncanny ability to find acorns, and in abundant years, the mast falls like rain." Chuck gestures toward the hills, where the tree canopy is so dense it nearly blocks out the sky. Released into the woods at just the right time, the pigs will fatten on nature's bounty, gobbling up acorns and nuts, and be ready for harvest before the heavy snows of winter.

In theory, it all makes perfect sense. But as Chuck reminds me, it's the small details that sometimes sabotage success, and without superior woodland genetics, the puzzle can quickly fall to pieces. To that end, Bert and Ernie have each been penned with two sows for a month, and today, thirty consecutive date nights have come to an end. Assistants Steve and R.D. coax Bert through a gate with a bucket of grain, into an alley where Chuck showers handfuls of cracked corn to keep him distracted. Before long, they've loaded the sows onto the low trailer, and Bert is back in his bachelor pad; the same routine goes for Ernie. Minutes later the sows are being trundled to their farrowing area, four rustic A-frame structures where the piglets will be born—by standard gestation, three months, three weeks, and three days from now.

Chuck affectionately scratches Bert behind the ear, then glances at his wristwatch.

"Whoops. I told Nadine we'd be in for a late breakfast, not late *for* breakfast." We head uphill to the cabin, where the warm smell of biscuits and bacon greets us at the front door. Inside, Nadine has prepared a platter of crisp bacon and a pan of steaming biscuits, placed beside a jar of homemade blueberry jam. We sit down to a midmorning feast of savory pork and sweet, buttery biscuits, washing it all down with a cup of strong black coffee.

Nadine and Chuck met in North Carolina, while he was still a professor at A&T. "My daughter convinced me to buy a little farm in a town called Silk Hope," Nadine recounts in a Carolina drawl. "And before I knew it, people were whispering: 'You know, there's a single man living across the road . . . and he's a *professor*!'"

She glances Chuck's way. "At first I was like, 'What*ever*.' But one day I decided I'd check him out, you know? And would you believe, that very day he came walking across the road, carrying tomatoes and figs . . . and flowers. Coming to meet

Chuck's Farming Wisdom

"The most important thing with livestock is constant contact from the farmer, the Temple Grandin style of benevolent caregiving. When you call the hogs, there's got to be fresh pasture, lots of food. Always good things happening."

the new neighbor." Nadine winks dramatically, and I notice Chuck blushing straight through his thick, white beard. "I mean, that was kind of *it*, right?"

They've been partners ever since. For ten years the couple has worked to create the ultimate acorn-finished pig, turning the fat of the land into the fat on the ham, an artisanal alchemy prized by chefs worldwide. It's the fat, after all, that's key to beautiful pork—a thick rind not only ensures flavor but also locks in moisture during the two-year curing process. Nadine and Chuck work with a partner to sell their hams to restaurants, slowly expanding as more chefs rave about their products.

Chuck ceremoniously rises from the table, unfurling a white cloth. There, held aloft in a wooden vise, is a solitary, prized, acorn-finished ham. It might be my imagination, but in the distance I suddenly hear a celestial choir ringing through the wooded hills.

In three deft slices the meat is plated, transparently thin and curled at the edges like a pink rose petal. Exquisitely salty and profoundly rich, the pork melts on my tongue like communion bread, palpable for an instant, then gone forever. My taste buds are delighted, craving more. I finish the slices with a balancing bite of biscuit, savoring the woody traces of walnut and hickory.

Grazed on hand-sown grain, finished on autumn acorns, Chuck might have invented a culinary fusion all his own: Spanish Allegheny. An ocean apart, perhaps, yet tantalizingly similar.

After breakfast, we climb the rough road that transects the farm, ducking beneath the supple limbs of pawpaw and hemlock, wild apples inherited from lost homesteads. Here, where the trail is too steep for work boots and the laurel too dense to pass, hogs will be loosed in a month's time, foraging for sustenance, a distant perimeter fence their only impediment.

We stand wordlessly, surveying our circumference. The land here is old, sacrosanct, silent in the dappled shade of summer. A thousand acorns born into a thousand oaks, time surpassing all understanding. Light bends everywhere—untenable, wild. A farm like Black Oak Holler is tamed only where clashing mountaintops intersect with startling blue sky.

Did You Know?

In the wild, pigs form a protective "sounder"—adults on the outside and piglets on the inside—in essence circling the wagons to watch for predators as they forage.

ANYTIME BISCUITS

From Black Oak Holler Farm

Makes 8 large or 12 medium biscuits

2 cups unbleached all-
purpose flour

2½ teaspoons baking powder

½ teaspoon baking soda

½ teaspoon salt

8 tablespoons (1 stick) very
cold unsalted butter (or lard,
if available)

⅔ to 1 cup whole buttermilk

Biscuits don't have to be relegated to breakfast—try these with some freshly cut ham and cheese for a quick lunch, dinner, or snack. The leftovers are even better the next morning when you split them in half, toast them, and then top them with some fruit preserves (such as the Blood Orange Marmalade on page 253).

1. Preheat the oven to 425°F.

2. Place the flour, baking powder, baking soda, and salt in a food processor and process to blend. Cut the butter into very small pieces, then add to the dry ingredients and process for 10 to 15 seconds, until well incorporated.

3. Transfer the mixture to a bowl and add ⅔ cup of the buttermilk. Using a wooden spoon, stir just until a dough forms. Add more buttermilk if necessary to get the dough to stick together.

4. Scrape the dough onto a floured surface and, using your hands, gently flatten it out to a 1-inch thickness. Sprinkle the dough with flour as needed if it becomes too sticky.

5. Cut out the biscuits using a sharp biscuit cutter, aiming straight down and then back up—don't twist the cutter. Dip the biscuit cutter in flour to keep it from sticking if necessary. Press the dough scraps together and pat it out, then cut additional biscuits from the remaining dough.

6. Place the biscuits in a baking dish and bake for 12 to 15 minutes, depending on the size, until golden brown on top. Let them cool in the pan for 5 minutes, then turn out and serve.

MUSTARD-BRAISED PORK SHOULDER

WITH FRIED CORNBREAD

Serves 4 to 6

Kick this meal up a notch by serving the pork shoulder with cooked greens, such as the Full-Flavored Collard Greens (page 64), alongside the fried cornbread. Since braising the meat takes awhile, you should wait to make the sides until right before you want to eat.

MUSTARD-BRAISED PORK SHOULDER

From Heritage Hollow Farms

Inspired by Black Oak Holler Farm

1. Combine the dry ingredients in a small bowl. Coat the pork shoulder completely with the rub. Refrigerate overnight, or for up to 24 hours. Remove the roast from the refrigerator 1 hour prior to cooking.

2. Preheat the oven to 300°F.

3. Heat the oil in a large Dutch oven over medium heat. Add the onion and cook for 7 minutes, stirring occasionally, then remove the onion from the pot.

4. Add the pork shoulder to the Dutch oven and sear each side for 7 to 10 minutes. It should be brown, but not burnt. Turn the roast, then return the onion to the pot and add the stock.

5. Cover the pot and place in the oven. Cook for 5 hours, basting the pork shoulder every hour with pan drippings. Test the roast with a fork; you should be able to easily pull

3 tablespoons brown sugar

2 tablespoons sea salt

2 tablespoons mustard powder

1 teaspoon onion powder

1 teaspoon garlic powder

1 teaspoon cayenne pepper

1 teaspoon freshly ground black pepper

1 teaspoon Spanish paprika

1 teaspoon ground cumin

1 teaspoon ground coriander

One 4- to 5-pound bone-in pastured pork shoulder (Boston butt)

2 tablespoons grape seed oil

1 white onion, chopped

3 cups stock (chicken, beef, or pork)*

Fried Cornbread (recipe follows)

the meat apart. If necessary, return the roast to the oven and cook for 1 more hour, then re-test with a fork. Serve it with cornbread to help sop up the delicious juices.

*Make your own stock from the bones of pasture-raised meats, if possible; not only is homemade stock more nourishing, it is also a cost-effective use of pastured proteins.

FRIED CORNBREAD

From Black Oak Holler Farm

Serves 4 to 6

1 cup plain coarsely ground cornmeal

½ cup unbleached all-purpose flour

1 teaspoon salt

½ teaspoon baking powder

½ cup hot water

Splash of milk

Oil or butter for frying

1. Whisk the dry ingredients together in a bowl. Gradually add the water and stir to make a thick batter. Let sit for a few minutes to thicken, then stir in enough milk to make a batter the consistency of applesauce.

2. Pour oil into a large cast-iron skillet to a depth of ¼ inch and heat over medium-high heat. Dollop spoonfuls of the batter into the hot oil and fry until the first side is brown. Flip the cornbread over and fry the other side until crispy and golden brown. Remove from the pan and drain on paper towels. Repeat with the remaining batter.

BBQ SAUCE

From Black Oak Holler Farm

Makes about 3 cups

Try pairing this sauce with acorn-finished ribs, grass-fed beef brisket, free-range chicken wings, or the Wild Rice Meatballs on page 210.

1. Heat the oil in a large saucepan over medium heat. Add the onions and cook until translucent, about 5 minutes. Add the garlic, sugar, salt, pepper, and pepper flakes, and add Worcestershire sauce and hot sauce to taste. Cook a few more minutes, stirring frequently to prevent the garlic from burning. Add the apple cider vinegar and your desired amount of ketchup.

2. Reduce the heat and simmer for about 2 hours (it takes that long for the vinegar to mellow and blend with the other ingredients; you can cook it for longer if you wish to tone it down even more). If the sauce gets too thick, add additional vinegar and reduce the heat. Remove from the heat and add the butter. This should keep in the refrigerator for up to a week.

*Using less ketchup will result in a thinner, Eastern North Carolina–style sauce that's great on pulled pork. Adding more ketchup will make a thicker sauce that's good for grilled meats.

⅓ cup olive oil
⅓ cup minced onion
4 garlic cloves, minced
1 teaspoon brown sugar
½ teaspoon salt
¼ teaspoon freshly ground black pepper
¼ teaspoon red pepper flakes
Worcestershire sauce
Hot sauce
2 cups apple cider vinegar + extra as needed
Up to ⅔ cup ketchup*
1 tablespoon unsalted butter

10

NICK MUTO AND BACKSIDE BAKES

CAPE COD, MASSACHUSETTS

Sustainable fishing

///////////////////////////////

I t's just past five in the morning as Nick Muto guides his lobster boat, *The Lost*, through Chatham Harbor. Anchored overnight fifty yards offshore, he chugs toward the dock where I stand waiting. The clear sky is flecked with crystalline stars as we load fresh bait onto the deck: skate backs and dog-fish heads, pungent scraps from what Nick calls 'Cape Cod's next-generation fishery.' Behind us, headlights swim across the parking lot as Fitzy, his crew-mate, parks his truck near the dock and hops aboard. The mooring ropes are cast. Moments later, we're pushing eastward into the black Atlantic swells.

Cold spray strikes the windshield as Nick, thirty-four, turns an old-fashioned peg wheel. Broad-shouldered and barrel-chested, he cuts a heavy shadow in the tiny cabin; green lights from the instrument panel silhouette his clean-shaven head. "I grew up here, on the Cape," he says, eyes scanning the horizon as he speaks. "And I'm the only one out of my high school friends to become a fisherman. One thing's for sure: There's not a lot of young guys getting into commercial fishing these days."

It certainly doesn't help that codfish, eponymous to the Cape, have all but disappeared from the area. "Some people blame overfishing," Nick explains, turning the wheel starboard, avoiding a sandbar that's been gradually migrating across the harbor. "No doubt, that's a big part of it, and I've been down to Washington several times, speaking before Congress about sensible regulations.

"But what most people don't know is, because of climate change, all of a sudden we've got harbor seals." He arches his eyebrows. "I'm talking fourteen, fifteen *thousand* of them. When I was a kid, it was a big deal if you saw a single one. And guess what? They love to eat cod, too."

Nick is part of a new generation of sustainable fishermen pursuing seafood that's local, abundant, and can be caught without collaterally impacting other species—commonly known as by-catch. On this morning we're going lobstering, the lobster being one of a handful of "fish" that fits Nick's criteria.

"Lobster, dogfish, skate, little conchs we call whelk. But you've gotta piece your season together. The years of just cod fishing, where maybe you'd take a couple months off to fish for tuna . . . those days are over. Guys have to do a little bit of everything, some black bass, stripers, and that's on top of dogfish and lobstering. You follow the season, but you've gotta to be careful, too. Anything can be overfished, and history has a way of repeating itself."

He reaches past the wheel, turning a hand crank to operate the windshield wiper. "As far as climate change, yeah, it could push a lot of the species out, and that's a shame. But it could also bring new species in, you know? Southern fish. Hey, they caught a white marlin in the canal this year." He barks a disbelieving laugh. "That's unheard of—it's a tropical fish!"

We're past the harbor now, and the shore lights recede into the distance. He leans hard against the throttle, and twin wakes of foam purl behind the stern, frothy white against the glinting waves. *The Lost* is headed seven miles out, and making good time. It's not long before the shoreline is lost from sight, and it occurs to me that I'm suddenly dependent on the fisherman for my safe return, the coast too far away now to swim. That is, if I even knew the direction. Nick, however, doesn't bother to glance at the map.

"Yeah, you could say we're local," he chuckles. "Fitzy grew up in Chatham; I'm from Orleans, live in Brewster now. It's all right here, on the elbow." He raises an arm, mimicking the shape of the Cape. "I went to Framingham State, got a degree in business. Even as recently as then, I could make enough money cod fishing that I could take the winters off and go back to school. I learned most of what I know from an older fisherman, going out to sea with him whenever I was between semesters. But these days, there's only one, maybe two guys fishing cod, and the only reason they make any money is the price is sky-high."

He yells to Fitzy over the roar of the diesel. "Hey! Anybody catching brown fish these days?"

Fitzy ponders the question. "Maybe Grayson? Mitchell?"

Nick nods. "Exactly. Maybe two guys. It all fell apart hard, I'm talking just one, maybe two years ago. For decades, scientists told us the fishery was on the verge of collapse, but guys kept saying, 'No, no, there's fish over here, there's fish over there. We've got plenty of fish.' Now?" He glances my way. "They reduced the quota by seventy percent this year. But you know what? They could have raised it by two hundred percent. It doesn't matter . . . there's no codfish out here. Most of the cod at restaurants and groceries? It's imported from Iceland and Norway now."

Without my noticing it, dawn has arrived, a pink smudge across the distant horizon. The waves, already impossibly black, seem somehow darker with the contrast. Insistent swells break against the bow, rocking us side to side. Nick backs off the throttle, and the motor slows to a low rumble. There, barely visible in the gathering light, a pale foam buoy bobs sideways against our furling wake. Leaning over the water, Fitzy reaches out and hooks it with a gaff. A sinuous rope emerges from the depths, an inverse lifeline attending invisible lobster pots below.

Nick hoists the buoy over a steel pulley and the motor squeals, catching traction, spraying us with icy Atlantic salt water. From the gravelly depths of seventy, sixty, fifty feet the rope retracts, coiled in a soggy pile around the fishermen's boots. At last, a boiling swell and the cage breeches against the hull. Black water rushes from the pot, sturdy and stoic and brimming, I imagine, with glistening red lobsters. Fitzy and Nick manhandle the crate over the side and open the hatch.

Inside are three fist-size crabs, a furry brown sand dollar, and an empty bait box—lobsterless, to be sure. Unconcerned, Nick waives a dismissive hand.

"We had good luck here just yesterday, no more than a hundred feet away. The next pot'll be better."

The next pot, in fact, is even worse. Beside the empty bait box, a solitary rock crab seems positively vexed at being yanked from the comfortably briny depths. Nick corrals the crustacean, the size of a yarmulke, studying it for a moment before returning it to the ocean. Wordlessly, he begins hauling the third pot.

Then the fourth. And the fifth. As the sixth pot rises, the sun now peeking above the horizon, the fisherman's disappointment is palpable. Nick wipes his beard smooth, flinging water from his gloved fingertips. "This is where the frustration sets in," he says, only half joking. "But it's been a long time since we didn't cover the cost of our diesel. We've got six more lines to go. Gotta hedge our bets out here."

Each line, Fitzy explains, is linked to twenty pots apiece, spaced 150 feet apart. All told, the area canvasses a three-thousand-foot stretch of ocean bottom. Baited with skate and dogfish chum, the lobsters enter the crates through tapering holes, and once in, can't find their way out. Ideally, each pot holds four or five legal-size lobsters, a metric determined primarily by tail length. But there are exceptions.

"Yeah, the eggers," Nick explains. "Fertilized females. Every once in a while, you'll pull up this big lobster, but when you turn it over, the undertail is covered thick with roe. Thousands of little black eggs. Those, we always put back. No eggs, no lobsters, right?"

Did You Know?

It takes the average lobster six to seven years to grow to harvestable size, but if left in the wild they can grow up to four feet long, weigh close to forty pounds, and live for more than one hundred years.

As he's speaking, Fitzy guides the seventh pot onto the side rail. This time, eureka. Two shining lobsters have taken the bait, their claws raised at defensive angles, antennae like double-fisted bullwhips. Fitzy reaches in without hesitation, lifting the lobster by its back carapace. I ask if it hurts to be pinched, and his hand pauses midair.

"Does it hurt?" He raises a solitary eyebrow, John Belushi style. "They've got a crusher claw they use for breaking crabs in half. So, yeah. You don't want to get your finger caught in the wrong place."

A quick check of the tail with a measuring bracket, and *snap!*—claw band one—*snap!*—claw band two—*plunk! plunk!*—the lobsters are dropped into the saltwater holding tank. I peer into the crystal depths, where the two lobsters have retreated to opposite corners. It would take a lot of them, I realize, perhaps a couple hundred, to fill the entire tank.

The day quickly grows productive. A few more empty pots to be sure, but on the whole each trap contains two or three nicely sized lobsters. Contrary to my recollections, the shells are more black than red, nearly as dark as the morning waves themselves. An arabesque of olive greens and obsidian camouflages the shells, swirling to red highlights only at the very edge. "Their pigment is intended for cold water, not hot," Nick explains. "So when you cook them, the red's the only color that holds up. All the other colors fade away."

Line after line, cage after cage. The live well begins to fill, and suddenly I wonder if there will be enough room. The work is steady, and after each rope is pulled Fitzy rebaits the pots. Nick guides the boat into position and the first trap is pushed from the stern, followed one after the next like paratroopers leaping from a plane.

I mention the analogy to Nick. "Never was in the military, but I used to be a cage fighter back in the day." He says this good-naturedly, his Massachusetts brogue pronouncing the

Nick's Fishing Wisdom

"My advice for someone starting out? Be a crew guy for a few years. Learn what's what. Everybody's in a rush to get to the helm. But being responsible for a couple of lives, getting everyone home safely? You'd better be experienced."

word "fight-ah." "It was all for fun, you know? I used to compete a good bit, but I gave it up when I decided to have kids. Too dangerous."

Too dangerous? Pardon me, Captain, but fishing is among the most dangerous jobs on the planet. What'll be his next hobby, I wonder, jumping motorcycles over active volcanoes? Not surprisingly, he already has a plan, albeit one that's slightly less flamboyant.

"I started doing clambakes on the weekends. Catering, the whole deal. At first, it was just for family and friends, then somebody said, 'Hey, people would pay for this, you know?' It's a Cape Cod tradition, the clambake—where people get together to drink beers, meet their neighbors. I call my business Backside Bakes." Nick laughs. "Who knows? Maybe my shoreside business will end up supporting my lobstering habit."

Littorally and literally, I think, but I keep my puns to myself. The day has ended well: 195 lobsters from 140 pots. At current prices, it's a gross of around one thousand dollars. Deducting fuel, maintenance, transport, and payroll, Nick estimates he'll collect a modest profit for the day's work. After five years of being a captain, he'll use the money to chip away at old debt.

Hands steady on the peg wheel, he guides the vessel westward, opening full throttle. The bow slaps against the chop, rainbow fans of spray bursting against the prow. It's been seven hours since we departed, and Nick appears lost in thought. "There's no secrets anymore," he volunteers without prompting. "We understand the science, realize that things are changing out here. If you're gonna make a living fishing, you've gotta adapt, figure out a way to live in balance. Is one sustainable fisherman like me going to change the world?" He stares steadily over the wheel. "Nah. I don't have any illusions of that. But I'm doing what I love, and try to do it right. Who knows? Maybe it'll catch on."

Safe in the harbor, we crate the lobsters into Fitzy's pickup. He leans from the driver's-side window and gives a curt wave, off to the wholesaler a few miles away. From there, the lobsters will end up in grocery stores and restaurants, shipped to all corners of the country.

Standing in the parking lot I can still feel the ocean moving through me, sea legs galore, a West Virginia landlubber if ever there was. I consider, then quickly dismiss, the idea of raising free-range lobsters in the Shenandoah Valley.

Nick has already moored *The Lost*, one of a dozen fishing vessels anchored safely offshore. Waves lap the pebble-scattered beach, and the tang of salt saturates the air. In the distance, he descends into a rowboat, an oar in each hand, back bent against the tide. The world falls silent as I watch, seabirds wheeling, kelp nudging the splintered pilings.

Platinum-hued oars glide through the afternoon light. Long ago, I imagine, a fisherman roped the moon, and was pulled inexorably out to sea. But man is made of ash, as well as water. Nick leans into his work, rowing homeward. Ceaselessly, bow against the current, we are forever borne to the attending shore.

Nick on the Future of Fishing

"I'm optimistic about the future, at least from a lobstering standpoint. But you've got to be willing to change. There's a lot of fishermen who'll go out of business each year—that's just the facts. The ones who can adapt, especially with the way the climate's changing—I think those are the one's who'll do okay."

LOBSTER ROLL

From Heritage Hollow Farms

Inspired by Nick Muto and Backside Bakes

Serves 4 to 6

4 cups chopped cooked lobster meat

½ cup mayonnaise

¼ cup chopped scallions

2 small celery stalks, finely chopped

Juice of ½ lemon

Salt and freshly ground black pepper

4 to 6 hot dog buns, toasted

Hot sauce, optional

Combine all the ingredients except the buns and hot sauce in a large bowl. Spoon the mixture into the toasted buns. Add a touch of hot sauce for extra spice, if desired.

BACKSIDE GRILLED CLAMS

From Nick Muto and Backside Bakes

Serves 1 as a main course, or more as an appetizer

1. Preheat the grill to medium-high, or 400°F.

2. Place the clams, butter, garlic, and seasoning on a large sheet of heavy-duty aluminum foil and fold the foil to make a packet; seal tightly. Wrap in a second layer of foil and seal tightly again. (Make sure that there are no clams poking holes through the foil, as that will allow juices to escape during cooking.) Place the foil packet on the grill and cook for 25 minutes.

3. Pour the cooked contents, including the broth, into a bowl and serve with crusty bread for dipping into the juices.

10 littleneck clams
⅓ stick (2 tablespoons + 2 teaspoons) unsalted butter
1½ tablespoons minced garlic
1 tablespoon Italian seasoning
Crusty bread

TRADITIONAL BACKSIDE CLAMBAKE WITH LOBSTER

From Nick Muto and Backside Bakes

Makes 1 hearty serving

Beer for steaming (any kind will work; wheat ale is recommended)

8 ounces mussels

8 ounces steamers (soft-shell clams)

1 ear corn on cob

¼ Vidalia onion

1 medium red potato, quartered

4 ounces linguiça links (or other spicy sausage)

One 1½-pound lobster

Melted butter

The ingredient amounts listed below make enough for a single, hungry person, but they can easily be increased to serve more. A large pot's worth generally makes enough for about 4 people.

1. Fill a large pot with about ½ inch of beer. Add the mussels, steamers, corn, onion, potato, and linguiça. Cover the pot and steam over medium-high heat, until the potato is soft and tender.

2. Fill a second large pot with ½ inch of water, set a steamer basket in the pot, and bring the water to a boil. Add the lobster and steam for 10 to 12 minutes.

3. Serve with melted butter and strained broth from the clambake.

11

TEXAS HONEYBEE GUILD

DALLAS, TEXAS

Urban honey

////////////////////////////////////

It's afternoon rush hour in downtown Dallas, Texas, and several stories below me, traffic is buzzing. Climbing up the fire escape, I swing my leg over the final rung and step onto the roof. Even from a distance, the brilliant reflection from the glass skyscrapers is momentarily blinding, and I cling to my handhold for fear of vertigo. When my vision finally clears, black dots dancing in the foreground, I slowly realize I'm not seeing sunspots. Directly in front of me is a friendly swarm of bees, with Brandon Pollard standing calmly in the middle.

"Run your finger through this honeycomb," he says, holding forth a frame of amber beeswax. The wooden rectangle is elegantly thin, and as he turns it he reveals a thousand tiny hexagons of honey, each capped with a translucent dollop of wax. Sensing my reluctance to damage such beauty, he proffers the comb a second time. "You can't hurt it," he insists, leveling the frame like a golden platter. "Every bee has seventeen different jobs, from gathering pollen to serving the queen. Honeycomb repair is one of them. Trust me, they won't hold it against you."

I've never been one to pink-slip a honeybee, and I'm not about to start today. Following his orders, I slide my finger into the delicate comb, the sensation akin to a spoon cracking through crème brûlée. The honey is surprisingly dark, the color of molasses poured over cornbread. Dolloped onto my

tongue, there's no mistaking the taste of marigolds and dandelions, the floral bouquet balancing the heavy notes of dark sugar. The after-taste brings to mind red clover—clean and mellow with the lightest hints of thyme and cardamom. It's a treat, quite frankly, and unlike anything I've ever had the pleasure of sampling.

"That's Zip Code Honey," Brandon says proudly, smiling through the shadows of his keeper's mask. "Bees can only travel three to five miles, and this hive is in the heart of Dallas. So we know that this honey came from 75270, from the flower beds and weeds that grow right here."

He returns the frame to the hive, sliding it between identical racks. Honeybees circle his head like a corona, dipping and weaving through the summer air. "Isn't that amazing?" he marvels, talking as he works. "A little dandelion growing in the sidewalk, it's something we take for granted. But for the bees, that's food. Keeping those little flowers alive is so crucial."

It's more than a bit surreal, standing on a rooftop in downtown Dallas, eating honey straight from the hive. But this is a normal day for Susan and Brandon Pollard, urban beekeepers and educators who spend their time wrangling honeybees all across the Dallas metro area. The couple maintains one hundred fifty hives in more than fifty different locations, selling the honey at

Dallas farmers' markets, food co-ops, and online to earn a living. Like the bees themselves, gamboling through their orbits, Brandon and Susan are constantly on the move, traveling from one end of the sprawling city to the other.

"It's a seven-days-a-week job," Susan explains, when I ask her about her schedule. "With this many hives, someone always has to be on call. The phone rings off the hook after a big thunderstorm. 'Hello? Lightning split the tree in my yard, and it's full of honeybees. Will you guys come get them?'" Her voice is languid, tranquil, much like Brandon's movements around the bees. "Most of the time, these callers are frightened, scared they're going to get stung. But there's really nothing to worry about. With honeybees, it's like meeting an unfamiliar dog: No sudden moves, and remain calm. If everything goes right, pretty soon you've made a new friend. No bites, and no stings. Come on," she adds gently. "Let's go visit some hives."

Today, I get to be a bee. We crowd into Brandon's black Chevy pickup, a battered five-speed with empty frames rattling in the bed. He pops the clutch and the truck lurches forward, puttering exhaust as he gears up to overdrive and accelerates onto I-35.

Most plants depend on pollinators to reproduce, ferrying living pollen from flower to flower, and honeybees are among the best in the business. Each spring, thousands of hives are loaded onto tractor trailers and trucked all over the country, hustled to almond blooms in California, or peach blossoms in Georgia. Once there, the bees are released to feed on flower nectar and pollinate the trees, which satisfies them for a month or two. But as soon as the blossoms fade, back onto the truck they go, whisked down the interstate to another location.

Brandon grimaces. "You've got to feel bad for them. When I was first learning how to keep bees, I rode on a few of those trucks, helped with hive deliveries. The mortality is just tremendous. Huge numbers die during transport. When you think about it, shipping bees coast-to-coast to propagate

Did You Know?

An average colony consists of twenty thousand to sixty thousand honeybees and one queen. An average worker bee (also known as a "maiden") produces one-twelfth of a teaspoon of honey during its six-week life span.

Brandon's Beekeeping Wisdom

"There are too many bee owners and not enough bee *keepers*," Brandon says. "Did you know you can order honeybees on Amazon? By definition, bees aren't personal property. They're nature."

thousand-acre monocultures, crops that need sprays and chemicals in the first place . . ." He trails off, momentarily at a loss for words. "It's just bizarre, you know? There's nothing sustainable about any of it."

These days, honeybee advocacy is always in the front of Brandon's mind. Back in college, however, bee farming in Texas couldn't have been farther from his radar. An all-American soccer player at the University of Virginia, as well as a US Olympian, he was drafted with the third pick of the Major League Soccer draft to the Dallas Burn in 1995. Then, in 1999, a devastating tackle from behind shattered his leg. Everyone thought his career was over.

Defying the odds, he spent an entire year rehabbing and eventually worked his way back onto the field. But on the second go-round, something felt lacking. "All of a sudden, I just didn't see the purpose in kicking a ball for entertainment. I

wanted to accomplish more, do something really meaningful with my life." Bucking all convention, he retired from professional soccer and went to work at a bakery.

"Yeah." He nods, as if it was the most logical decision in the world. "When I was playing, I met a baker who made this incredible, healthy bread. But the guy was just killing himself, working way too hard. So it made sense to me to help him, you know? That's how I got this truck," he says, patting the steering wheel. "And how I met Fluffy, too."

"Fluffy?" I repeat.

"Yeah, Susan," Brandon affirms. "Fluffy, Queen Bee, I've got a lot of nicknames for her. Meeting her changed my life. Got me healthy, made me whole. When I retired from soccer, people say I traded money for honey." He grins, showing off an even row of beautiful teeth. "Sounds good to me."

There's no denying that Brandon, forty-one, and Susan, sixty-two, make an unconventional pairing. Susan's background is in holistic healing, and when the couple met, she was running a center focused on natural, restorative health. She laughs at the memory.

"Of course, after his injury it was no surprise that he came to see me," Susan recalls. "We had already been introduced by mutual acquaintances long before that. Eventually, a close friend told us, 'You know, you guys make such a beautiful couple.' We didn't realize it at first, but over time we'd totally fallen for each other. It took someone else to see it for us."

It's a mystery, how certain people notice things that others never see at all. That's precisely what Susan and Brandon now do for a living, speaking up for an insect that can't speak for itself. Dubbing themselves "beevangelists," they're ambassadors for honeybees in a landscape populated with skyscrapers, subdivisions, and SUVs.

Brandon's Bee Humor

"People say we're evangelists. We say we're *bee*vangelists. Hey, if you don't like our sense of humor, you can buzz off."

"It's just crazy," Susan says, "the amount of spraying that's gone on here the past few years. Due to the West Nile virus, they send out airplanes to fog the city with insecticide. It's supposed to kill mosquitos, but of course it's devastating to the bees as well. So when the alert goes off—usually late at night—that's when we jump in the truck, and rush into action."

The alert, given in advance of spraying to encourage people to stay indoors, is Brandon and Susan's cue. Into the battered pickup they go, sprinting across the city to cover their beehives with tarps. It's all a fervent effort to keep the defenseless honeybees from being asphyxiated by the poison. According to Texas A&M's website, their concerns are not unmerited: "It is likely that at least some insect species . . . may be harmed, at least temporarily, by mosquito spraying."

Susan sighs. "Look, it's impossible to measure the damage done by this spraying. But we do know one thing. Across the country, colony collapse disorder—that's what it's called when a hive inexplicably dies—is at thirty-three percent. In Dallas? It's at *sixty* percent. Is there a connection?" She spreads her palms. "All I can say is, we're going to keep protecting our bees the best way we know how."

Brandon parks near a backyard garden in the suburbs, where nights before the couple had tarped the hives against insec-

ticide at two in the morning. He lights the smoker, producing ethereal white plumes. The billowing smoke keeps the bees sedate by masking their alarm pheromones. "I usually use sage and rosewood, because it smells so nice," he says. "But sometimes I'll shred my credit card bills, and put them in there, too. That's especially therapeutic."

On this morning, all seems well. The bees have survived the West Nile spraying and are busy at work gathering pollen. All at once, however, Brandon pauses.

"Uh-oh, Fluff. Looks like we've got a false queen trying to take the throne." He lifts a frame from the box. Typically, the honeycomb is a uniform prairie of repeating identical hexagons. On this comb, however, there's a noticeable aberration, a turgid nodule rising conspicuously above the golden plain.

"Can't have that," Brandon says matter-of-factly, not hesitating as he scoops it away with an index finger. "The hive got confused," he explains, "because we introduced a new queen this spring. But if there's no queen for a month or so—as was the case here—the colony will raise one themselves. It's a mixture of pheromonal signals, and the special way they're fed."

He raises his finger, where thick, yellowy-white honey glistens in the morning light. "This is called royal jelly, the food of the queens, a real delicacy. Here," he says, holding it out.

"Try it."

How can I say no? I swipe the gooey glob from his finger and pop it into my mouth. Sweet, certainly, but intensely tangy, akin to the taste of fresh Greek yogurt. Chewing, I also detect something altogether different, an earthy bitterness that I can't quite identify. I swallow and find Brandon staring at me admiringly.

"You're so brave to eat the larva! Most people pick it out."

The queen maggot. An earthy—and chewy—bitterness. Yes, I tell myself, that was the taste. That was it exactly.

Moments later, we're off yet again. Dallas is a city where *fútbol* is respected, but football is king. As such, it's startling to see goalposts rising from rows of collard greens, a one-hundred-yard garden in what was clearly once a football field. But that's the scene at Paul Quinn College, one of dozens of community gardens Brandon and Susan service with their hives.

"When we first started," Susan recounts, "we were these odd little beekeepers making cold calls. We'd visit restaurants, hotels, anywhere we could get high visibility to stress the importance of pollination. 'Would you like some bees on your rooftop?' we'd ask. At first, chefs and CEOs thought we were crazy. Bees on the rooftop, in the middle of the city?" She smiles. "Now, we can't keep up with the requests. Once the Omni found out the Fairmont had bees, well guess what? Now they're ready to play catch-up."

She pauses, regarding the repurposed football field, filled to overflowing with kale and Swiss chard. "You know, I've lived here for forty-five years, and if there's one thing you can say about Texas, it's this: We always want to be the best. There's tremendous state pride here, you can see it everywhere you go. It's just like the old saying: 'Everything's bigger in Texas.'

"But when it comes to agriculture," she continues, "we're getting left behind. All the focus is on huge crops of monocultures. Corn, cotton, soybeans. But how can they forget the pollinators, the ones that make most of our food possible?" Susan studies me with pale blue eyes, searching for an answer. "Texas could be leading the nation in sustainable agriculture. Instead, we're falling behind. What a missed opportunity."

Brandon doffs his beekeeper's hat and kisses Susan's cheek. "The answer is so simple," he adds. "It's food. Forage. Stop spraying our lawns with herbicide. What's natural about a lawn laced with chemicals, anyway? Do we really need to blast every dandelion and clover bud with poison?"

It's easy to imagine these words as confrontational, provocative, angry. But as I listen to Brandon, his tone is earnest, his questions coming from a world-weary heart. "In some neighborhoods I've visited, there's nothing for the bees to eat, not a single wildflower." He shakes his head, not with sadness or frustration, but with wonder.

"Who doesn't like honey? Please, lay off the spraying. Let's leave some food for the bees."

HONEY-ORANGE DRUMSTICKS

From the Texas Honeybee Guild

Makes 3 dozen drumsticks, with enough extra sauce for dipping

HONEY-ORANGE SAUCE

2 tablespoons toasted sesame oil

1 teaspoon chopped fresh ginger

1 teaspoon chopped garlic

¾ cup water

¾ cup local honey

¼ cup fresh orange juice + extra to taste

3 tablespoons fresh lemon juice + extra to taste

3 tablespoons fresh lime juice

1 tablespoon soy sauce

Pinch of red pepper flakes

1 cinnamon stick

2 tablespoons cornstarch dissolved in 3 tablespoons cold water

3 dozen chicken drumsticks

Salt and freshly ground black pepper to taste

2 tablespoons sesame seeds, toasted

4 scallions, sliced

2 tablespoons orange zest

This citrusy yet savory, sweet-and-sour take on drumsticks was provided to the Texas Honeybee Guild by chef Jason Weaver at the Omni Hotel in Dallas. If you like, you can use chicken wings instead of drumsticks.

1. Preheat the oven to 375°F. Season the drumsticks with salt and pepper. Bake the drumsticks on a rimmed baking sheet or dish for 15 to 20 minutes, until their internal temperature reaches 165°F when tested with a meat thermometer.

2. While the drumsticks bake, make the sauce: Heat the oil in a large skillet over medium heat. Add the ginger and garlic and sauté until fragrant. Add the water, honey, orange juice, lemon juice, lime juice, soy sauce, pepper flakes, and cinnamon stick and bring to a boil.

3. Slowly pour the cornstarch mixture into the boiling liquid to thicken it, whisking constantly. (Note: If the liquid is not boiling it will not thicken. If the sauce doesn't reach the correct consistency, you can make more of the cornstarch and cold-water mixture and whisk in a bit to help tighten things up. The consistency of the sauce should be similar to a sweet-and-sour sauce, a little thick so it will stick to the drumsticks.)

4. Add orange juice and lemon juice to taste. Remove the cinnamon stick.

5. Toss the drumsticks with the Honey-Orange Sauce and garnish with sesame seeds, scallions, and orange zest.

TIP:

These are also great fried. To fry them, heat a layer of oil in a deep pan or set your deep fryer to 325°F and slowly cook them until they're crispy on the outside and cooked through in the center; their internal temperature should reach 165°F when tested with a meat thermometer.

HONEY-BOURBON ICE CREAM

From the Texas Honeybee Guild

Makes 1 to 1½ quarts ice cream

A sophisticated ice cream to enjoy on a hot summer day, this recipe came to the Texas Honeybee Guild from Chef April Barney of Skyline High School's Culinary Arts Department in Dallas.

1 cup whole milk
¾ cup local honey + extra for garnish
6 egg yolks
½ cup sugar
1 cup heavy cream
¾ cup bourbon*

1. Heat the milk in a medium saucepan over medium-high heat to the scalding point, being careful not to scorch it. Set aside.

2. Using a mixer with the whip attachment, whip together the honey, egg yolks, and sugar until light in color. With the mixer on low speed, slowly add the hot milk to the egg mixture and mix until thoroughly combined. (Be careful not to add the milk too quickly or the eggs will begin to cook.)

3. Return the mixture to the saucepan and cook over low heat, stirring constantly, until thick enough to coat the back of a spoon. Remove from the heat and let the mixture cool until it's warm but not hot to the touch.

4. Add the heavy cream, then the bourbon, and mix thoroughly. Transfer the mixture to a container with a lid and refrigerate until completely cooled.

5. Remove the chilled mixture from the refrigerator and freeze with an ice cream machine, following the manufacturer's instructions.

6. Drizzle with honey before serving.

*Look around your area for some locally crafted bourbon or whiskey.

SPRING DANDELION SALAD

WITH CANDIED WALNUTS AND CITRUS VINAIGRETTE

From Heritage Hollow Farms

Inspired by Texas Honeybee Guild and all honeybees everywhere

Serves 2 to 4

CANDIED WALNUTS

1 cup walnuts

1 tablespoon coconut oil

¼ cup sugar

½ teaspoon cinnamon

CITRUS VINAIGRETTE

¼ cup fresh orange juice (4 to 5 oranges)

½ cup olive oil

¼ cup apple cider vinegar

Salt and pepper to taste

2 tablespoons orange zest (1 orange)

FRIED DANDELION BLOSSOMS

Oil for cooking

1 egg

2 tablespoons almond meal or flour

Pinch of sugar

Pinch of salt

1 cup dandelion blossoms, divided*

1 pound spinach

½ cup radishes

½ cup blueberries

CANDIED WALNUTS

Combine walnuts, oil, sugar, and cinnamon over low heat, stirring frequently for approximately five minutes until sugar has melted. Toss and spread out on a baking sheet coated in parchment paper. Set aside.

CITRUS VINAIGRETTE

Combine fresh orange juice with olive oil, apple cider vinegar, salt, and cracked pepper. Zest one orange over the mixture. Whisk together and set aside to allow flavors to combine. Note: You will have approximately 16 ounces of dressing with plenty to store in the fridge.

FRIED DANDELION BLOSSOMS

1. Heat oil in a small fry pan over low heat. Whisk the egg in a bowl. Combine flour, sugar, and salt in another bowl. Place ½ cup of dandelion blossoms in the egg wash and then transfer to the flour mixture. Gently fry in oil until lightly brown. Transfer to a plate and set aside.

2. Rinse and chop the spinach. Thinly slice the radishes (a microplane works well for uniformly thin slices). Combine the spinach, radishes, fried and fresh dandelion blossoms, candied walnuts, and blueberries. Drizzle with vinaigrette. Enjoy out in the sunshine!

TIP:

Leave out the fried blossoms and simply use fresh. Add in dandelion greens for a more bitter bite or foraged chickweed for a softer flavor. This is a great dish for kids to help with.

*Please don't use any dandelions that have been sprayed with weed-killing chemicals. Dandelions are a favorite for pollinators so think twice before removing them all from your yard. Instead, share them with the bees!

12

KIYOKAWA FAMILY ORCHARDS

PARKDALE, OREGON

Pears, peaches, cherries, and apples

The cherries are ready. Fruit is begging to be picked, plump red clusters glinting with afternoon sunshine, a delicate fragrance sweetening the air between rows of trees. Buckets strapped at chest level, workers busily pick Rainiers, glorious yellow globes blushing with pink hues, bashful as a schoolboy passing a valentine. There's a low rumble as the fruit is tipped into white receiving crates, a landslide of cherries bouncing and tumbling, seeking their angle of repose. Ladders are pivoted like protractors, and not a cluster is left behind. Tomorrow morning, the streets of Portland will be festooned in fruit, the farmers' market decorated with irresistibly sweet cherries.

In a valley famous for its pears, it's the cherries that must be picked. Today.

"That's the beauty of having an orchard," says Randy Kiyokawa, fifty-three, appraising the day's harvest. "The fruit is picked at the peak of freshness, the exact moment it's ready to eat." He snaps a pair of Lapins from a branch, twin rubies flecked with rose highlights, displaying them in his palm. "But it's also part of the challenge. We've got exactly five days to get these picked. Will my crew be ready? Are the tractors going to start? What if it rains two days straight?" He studies the cherries thoughtfully, then gently drops them in the bin. "It takes a certain personality to grow fruit for a living, that's for sure."

A third-generation orchardist, Randy has spent a lifetime balancing risk and reward. The Hood River Valley, where his grandfather settled a

hundred years earlier, thrusts contrast directly into the landscape: Crowned with snow, robed in rock, Mount Hood is a regal reminder of the beauty—and peril—of living so closely linked to nature. The mountain erupted as recently as the early 1800s, and occasional tremors are still felt to this day.

On the edge of his orchard, where newly trellised apple trees are supported by bamboo and juniper posts, the valley abuts a stories-high avalanche of impenetrable black rock. This is an ancient pyroclastic flow, formerly red-hot rocks that seared a path of oblivion across the valley floor. Centuries later, only a smattering of evergreens have managed to penetrate the austere terrain. Randy gestures to the towering wall of stones.

"In a way, it's the best thing that could have happened for our orchard. When we decided to go organic, we needed a place where we could be free of pesticide drift, potential contamination that's carried on the wind. This is a sheltered spot, a haven, protected by nature itself."

Organic production is a new venture for Kiyokawa Family Orchards, but one that Randy is eagerly embracing. "We've always been minimum-spray farmers. That's just common sense. Do you remember the Alar scare, back in the late eighties? We didn't even use the stuff, but boy, did we feel the consequences. And packing houses that normally bought our fruit, well, that year they made us pay *them* to take it. Fifty dollars a load just to throw it away—to make it go away—and our apples weren't even sprayed with the stuff." He sighs, the pain still evident even decades later. "A lot of orchards went under after that. It was a hard time in the valley. But our farm pulled through."

Like an orchard itself, where a cold snap can destroy a spring bloom or a summer drought can wither harvests on the branch, the Kiyokawa family has weathered decades of challenges beyond their control. Having emigrated from Japan in 1905, Randy's grandfather Riichi found a job as a railroad worker before recognizing an opportunity to grow fruit in the fertile valley below Mount Hood. He bought a small parcel of land in 1911 and slowly began to grow his farm, marrying his wife, Rae, and starting a family along the way. It took ten years for the orchard to mature into production, and he intrepidly planted asparagus and strawberries between the rows, creating revenue while buying time. By 1940 he had established himself as a successful farmer, widely respected as one of the top producers in the region.

Then came World War II, and with it a crushing wave of xenophobia. More than one hundred thousand Japanese Americans were driven into internment camps, Riichi and his family included. Forced by the federal government to abandon their orchard, they were rounded up as prisoners of war. With little time to spare, Riichi quickly contacted several white farming peers, imploring them to hold his land in trust until

Randy on Farming Trends

"They say the West Coast is usually ahead with trends, but it's the East Coast that's taken the lead on hard cider. We're now planting lots of cider-apple varieties, and it's people from the east who are coming out here to make it."

Randy's Farming Wisdom

"In a way, farming is like being an artist with a blank canvas. There's so much I want to grow, so much I'd like to see. Farmers use land to project their ideas."

he might someday return to reclaim it. They gave him their word that they would.

Dark times followed. Many Japanese American farmers lost their land forever, acreage that was seized and sold at rock-bottom prices to profiteering speculators. Randy considers his own family to be extremely fortunate.

"My grandfather had the good luck to find trustworthy men, farmers who not only tended his land but returned it to him after he was released. There were plenty of farmers who were cheated out of their property, people who broke their promises and stole the orchards outright. It's a black eye on history around here. But my grandfather's friends kept their integrity, even if they didn't have to. It was a lesson he passed down to us when we were kids."

After years of incarceration in the prison camp, Randy's father joined the US Army and was assigned to be a translator in Japan after the war. He returned home in 1951 to purchase property of his own, not far from the family homestead. This is where Randy and his four sisters were raised, in a land of gently rolling hills, aproned around the waist of Mount Hood itself.

"You know, growing up, I wasn't really sure I wanted to go into farming. Of course, I've got it in my genes; there's no denying that. But after I got home from Oregon State, I thought maybe I'd be a police officer, or a disc jockey." He laughs. "People always say I've got the perfect face for radio."

But it was farming that won the day. Randy returned home to a legacy of familiar abundance, a heritage of pears and peaches, cherries and apples. "Back then, it was Japanese tradition that the first son take over the farm," he explains. "Of course, now we know that women farm just as well as men, oftentimes even better. But since I was the first son—even though I'm the youngest child overall—that's the hand I was dealt."

Randy leads me down an aisle of Bartlett pears, the silver trunks twisting as gracefully as a dancer's waist. At eighteen hundred feet the orchard is among the highest in the valley, its high altitude bringing a seasonal ballet that comes with its own rewards and challenges.

"We're usually about three weeks behind everyone else, because the elevation keeps us cooler. That can be helpful, stretching out the season a bit, having fruit at market when the other growers are done for the year. On the other hand," he adds, "it can backfire. Just when everyone is sick of eating peaches, we say, 'Oh, look! We've got truckloads of peaches!'" He laughs, tipping back his cap. "Sometimes, it's just impossible to win."

Even so, Randy's farming optimism speaks for itself. We climb into an old pickup, passing an eighty-acre parcel where he recently signed a long-term lease: twenty-five years to grow more fruit. For most businesses, a quarter of a century is considered a lifetime, two and a half decades of development, marketing, expansion, and maturity. With orcharding this timeline can feel glacial, incomprehensibly slow, a never-ending game of hurry up and wait. Thinking of growing apples? The rewards can be delayed for a decade.

"We signed the lease in March," Randy recounts, pulling the truck to the side and climbing out of the cab. "And by April, we were putting in trees. Apples, pears, cherries, whatever we could get in the ground. Five thousand young saplings. Since it's only a twenty-five-year lease, we had to get going quick."

The results are astonishing. Before us fifty rows of waist-high trees stretch toward the horizon, branches blending into the distant, hazy foothills. Gridded like graph paper, five thousand trees is more than just a number. It's a testament, a tangible declaration of faith. I quickly run the numbers. This commitment will carry the farmer well into his eighties, and beyond.

KA-*BOOM*!

I jump straight out of my skin. An explosion like a howitzer rocks the tranquil morning, sending birds into flight from nearby trees. Momentarily deafened, I turn to Randy for an explanation.

"Yeah," he says sheepishly. "The cannon. Sorry about that, forgot to tell you. When you hear the little click, you've got to cover your ears."

I notice it now, a silver cylinder on a tripod, with a black hose looping to a white propane pony. "It's one of the tools in our organic toolbox, a gunshot noise to scare away birds." He nods toward the contraption, considering. "Funny thing is, though, the birds get used to it after a while. Before, they would fly in and eat an entire piece of fruit. Now, they'll peck a little bit at one, get scared away, then fly to a different tree, peck on a different piece." He spreads his hands helplessly. "There's no easy solutions with anything. Organic, conventional . . . they all come with unique challenges."

Take weeds, for example. Instead of spraying herbicide, the farmer keeps noxious plants in check with strips of geo-textile fabric, heavy layers of cloth that prevent sunshine from reaching undesired vegetation. Each week or so the fabric is moved to a new strip, leaving the soil beneath the trees effectively weeded. Better yet, it has the double benefit of exposing subterranean pests, namely root-hungry voles.

"Yeah, mice and voles really tear us up, eating the sweet roots of young trees. But if we can reduce weed pressure, clearing up the sight lines, then natural predators can help us out. Hawks, kestrels, even garter snakes. Simple things like this can really improve produc—"

On the periphery of consciousness, I hear a soft click. Quick as I can, I cover my ears.

KA-*BOOM*!

His own ears protected, Randy nods his approval. Evidently, I'm learning how to be an organic orchardist.

"—production," he concludes. "And with organic farming, we've got to use every trick we've got."

I can empathize with the pests. After all, who—or what— wouldn't enjoy a chemical-free peach, cherry, or apple? It was all right there for the taking. I had already eaten a handful of cherries myself that morning, and even those had practically fallen off the tree and into my mouth.

Randy on Economic Realities

"Look, my dad used to get ten cents a pound for his pears, back in the sixties. You know what we get today, fifty years later, on the open market? Thirteen to fifteen cents a pound. Fifty years, with a nickel raise. Orchardists go out of business each year trying to make it."

The heart of the farm is one hundred and seven acres of pear trees, limbs heavy with clusters of gorgeous purple fruit.

"These are Seckels," the farmer says, holding out a cluster of dark, kiwi-size pears. "Very sweet, perfect for a lunch box. We raise Anjou, Butler, Bosc . . . about twenty-five varieties in all. See, it's the apples, cherries, and peaches that go to farmers' markets, but ninety-eight percent of my pears get sent to a processor, to be canned. At weekend markets, the other fruit outsells the pears ten to one. Still, we try to stay diversified, and at this elevation, pear trees are the best at resisting cold snaps."

He pauses, reflecting. "When it comes to farming, desperation can have a big influence. Take our roadside stand for example. Back in the eighties, fruit prices were so bad, we barely covered our cost of picking. It was 1987, and we needed an alternator on the tractor, sixty-eight dollars. I can still remember asking myself, 'Where will the money come from? How can I possibly afford sixty-eight dollars?'"

We pass between rows of mature trees, the warm scent of pears perfuming the air. "It was a cold, rainy November that year, and I had picked a crate of Red Delicious apples, putting a sign along the road: APPLES, 5¢ A POUND." Randy laughs humorlessly at the memory. "Yeah, five cents! And if they bought the entire box, I'd drop it to three." He kicks at the leaves, head lowered. "I probably wasn't a very good marketer. But what I did do was listen. Listen to what the customers told me."

Reaching the end of the row, Randy stops at the rough, graveled road that bisects the farm. A tractor rolls past with a forkload of fruit, white bins filled with freshly harvested pears. The farmer stands with his forearms crossed over his chest.

"That year," he continues, "a customer asked me to plant Golden Delicious. So the following spring, I did. Then in the early nineties, someone suggested Honey Crisp, a variety I'd never even heard of. Boy"—he winks—"that worked out well. A year or two later, a family asked if their kids could pick fruit out in the orchard, so we started a pick-your-own. And when my friend Joe got out of farmers' markets, he offered me his locations. That's how we wound up selling in Portland."

Orcharding is replete with fruit idioms, expressions we've all heard a million times. *Life is a bowl of cherries. Everything is peachy-keen.* But for a multigeneration pear farmer, the offerings are surprisingly sparse. *Comparing pears and oranges?* No way. *One bad pear spoils the bunch?* Never heard it. Grain farmers suffer with corny clichés, and dairy jokes are reliably cheesy. But when it comes to fruit, pears always play second banana.

It's probably a lucky thing, though. Randy's family has created its own definitions of success, expressing themselves through a landscape of blossoms and bending boughs. For one hundred ten years, three generations of Kiyokawas have faced challenges and risks that, to many people, would seem unfathomable. And that, you might say, suits a farmer like Randy Kiyokawa just pearfectly.

SAVORY PEACH SOUP

From the Smith Meadows Kitchen

Inspired by Kiyokawa Family Orchards

Serves 10

1. Melt the butter in a large skillet over low heat. Add the onion and cook until the onion begins to turn translucent and brown, about 10 minutes. Add the white wine and port and cook until the liquid has reduced completely and the onion is caramelized, 5 to 10 minutes.

2. Place the onion in a large bowl and add the peaches, vinegar, and salt. Using an immersion blender, puree until ultra-smooth. You can also puree it in batches using a standing blender.

3. Serve immediately or refrigerate to enjoy later. It will keep for approximately 5 days.

8 tablespoons (1 stick) unsalted butter

½ large Vidalia onion, chopped

½ cup white wine

¼ cup port

4½ pounds peaches (or nectarines or other similar stone fruit; *not plums*), peeled, pitted, and chopped

3 tablespoons white vinegar

1 teaspoon salt

PEARADISE PIE

From Kiyokawa Family Orchards

Makes one 9-inch pie

One 9-inch pie shell, unbaked (recipe follows)

8 to 10 ripe Bartlett pears, peeled, cored, and thinly sliced

Juice of ½ lemon

4 tablespoons (½ stick) unsalted butter, at room temperature

¾ cup sugar

3 large eggs, at room temperature

1 teaspoon vanilla extract

⅛ teaspoon salt

¼ cup unbleached all-purpose flour

¼ teaspoon ground nutmeg or mace

Whipped cream, optional (see page 223 for Maple Whipped Cream)

1. Preheat the oven to 350°F.

2. Arrange the sliced pears in the pie shell in a layered pattern. Sprinkle the lemon juice over the fruit.

3. Cream the butter and sugar together in a medium bowl. Beat in the eggs, vanilla, and salt. Add the flour and mix until smooth.

4. Pour the mixture over the fruit, then lightly sprinkle the nutmeg over the top. Bake for 45 minutes, or until the filling is set and slightly brown.

5. Let the pie cool, then serve topped with whipped cream, if desired. This is best served on the day it is made. Refrigerate any leftovers. Note: You can also use 4 to 5 apples in place of half of the pears.

HOMEMADE PASTRY CRUST

1½ cups unbleached all-purpose flour

Pinch of salt

½ cup lard

3 to 4 tablespoons cold water

1. Combine the flour and salt in a large bowl. Add the lard and mix, using a pastry cutter or your fingers, until large crumbs form. Slowly sprinkle the cold water into the mixture, 1 tablespoon at a time, until the dough feels sticky enough to hold together. Gather the dough into a ball and refrigerate for 30 minutes.

2. Roll the chilled dough out on a lightly floured surface. Carefully wrap one edge of the crust over the length of a rolling pin and slowly roll the crust around the pin, then lift and gently unroll over a 9-inch pie plate. (Alternatively, you can pat the dough into a large circle and press it into the pie plate using your fingers.)

13

PAUL'S GRAINS

LAUREL, IOWA

Organic grains

Iowa is a sea of corn and soy. Placards, as friendly as yard-sale signs, promote colorful new varieties: AgriGold, Asgrow, DEKALB. Cornfields abut lawns at ninety-degree angles, the grass clipped to two pristine inches and the white houses lacquered with generations of paint. Grain is ubiquitous. Stalks stand stolid as soldiers, straight-backed and resolute beneath an expansive Midwestern sky. Windows down, radio singing—the air is floral with possibility.

There's no debating the beauty of the landscape, a rolling topography arrested by stop-signed crossroads, infinity available at each intersection. At turns austere, at turns sweetly inviting, towns reveal themselves like surnames in a phonebook. Baxter and Newton, Kellogg and Ferguson. Tradition is tangible, permanently pressed into the fabric of forearmed shirtsleeves.

In a nation where trucker hats and Carhartts have become mainstream fashion, Iowa flaunts a retro coolness anchored in authenticity. Vintage isn't so much a style as it is a lifestyle. But make no mistake. The corn and beans flanking the highways are the pinnacle of scientific technology, genetically modified organisms engineered to resist herbicides that decimate competing vegetation. The grain is developed in laboratories, patented as proprietary, and distributed by multibillion-dollar companies. It's illegal for farmers to retain seeds from these crops, putting a stop to a tradition as old as agriculture itself.

Did You Know?

Spelt has been cultivated by farmers since 5000 BCE. Though it contains gluten, the molecular structure of spelt is different from that of wheat, lending itself to easier digestion for many with wheat-gluten intolerance.

These contemporary realities make Paul's Grains an extraordinary throwback. On a hilltop overlooking kingdoms of corn, the farm is a hundred-acre organic oasis an hour northeast of Des Moines. Fields of rye bend into acres of buckwheat. Golden oats delta toward parcels of spelt. Turning into the driveway I spot Steve Paul, sixty, lithe as a stem of wheatgrass himself.

"It was my father, Wayne, who really changed things around here," the grain farmer says, an unadorned baseball cap topping his head. "When he got home from Iowa State, he was ready to go modern. Chemicals, fertilizer, machinery. All of it. At college, he had learned the latest methods and couldn't wait to improve my grandfather's old-fashioned farm."

Near the barns, laying hens scratch the dusty gravel for grit. The day is overcast and temperate, a gentle respite for a late July morning. Modest outbuildings flank the tidy barnyard, oak boards nailed to stout upright posts with swirled knotholes.

"Then," he continues, "after a few years, Dad began to change his mind, thinking maybe all these chemicals weren't as safe as the companies claimed. Not as healthy for the soil, or the farmers. So, in 1964, he decided to go organic. You could say he was a little ahead of his time."

To put the audacity of this move into perspective, in the early sixties, the term "organic farming" had barely been coined. Popularly attributed to Walter James's *Look to the Land*, published in 1940, organic farming was so obscure in the mid-twentieth century that it couldn't even be considered a trend. But Steve's father, Wayne, intuitively sensed modern farming practices had strayed from the path of sustainability. Lessons learned in the classroom didn't seem to add up out in the field. In short order, the farmer found himself a burgeoning pioneer, living in the land of Pioneer seed.

Steve, one of four children, was just a kid when this change was unfolding. Growing up on the farm, he watched as his father gradually adapted the business, tinkering with milling his own flour, using traditional stone wheels to grind grain into fine powder. Before long, Wayne began offering wheat, corn, and oat flours for sale—the farm's first attempts at directly selling to the public. Some years later, when the family introduced a seven-grain cereal and a pancake mix, the products ended up selling like, well . . . hotcakes. Clichés, after all, exist for a reason.

If selling homemade granola and hand-milled flour doesn't strike you as especially revolutionary, then we'd do well to remember the context of the setting. Throughout most of Iowa, grain is harvested straight onto trucks and hauled away, destined for livestock feed and ethanol production. To be sure, there are minor exceptions to this rule, such as high-fructose corn syrup production, and some farms must

Steve's Farm Humor

"When we bought a used tractor, I told the organic inspector, 'I let the old air out of the tires, and refilled them when I got to the farm.'" Steve laughs. "We only use organic air in our tractor tires."

certainly save some of their own grain for personal use. But in a land of commoditized big ag, where the Chicago Mercantile Exchange is as influential as Mother Nature herself, no one can argue that a small farm like Steve's steadfastly bucks the major trends.

The ability to remain flexible, to rotate and adapt, is the key to success at Paul's. In fact, it's a seasonal rotation of crops that ensures increased organic fertility, an intentional mimicry of nature to build balance into annual production.

"We start with oats, and put out alfalfa at the same time. Oats act as a nurse crop for the alfalfa, which we'll harvest as hay for three years. Next comes rye and wheat, followed by soybeans. Lastly, we'll come in with corn. The rotation takes a full decade to cycle through."

The secret to a ten-year rotation, Steve explains, is a unique grass-legume relationship. Soybeans and alfalfa, both legumes, have the natural ability to pull nitrogen out of the air,

fixing it deep within the soil. Grasses—namely wheat, rye, barley, and corn—can then utilize this as fertilizer, sending blades and seed heads up, and roots downward. More roots means more carbon, crucial for absorbing and retaining rainfall. For a grain farmer such as Steve, grasses and legumes are a match made in heaven. Or, in this case at least, a hundred heavenly acres in north central Iowa.

"Our corn is open-pollinated, which is quite different than the hybrid varieties, even the organic hybrids. Hybrids, you see, are bred for quantity; our corn is bred for *flavor*. Once you compare the two, you can taste the difference right away."

The grain is stored in wagons, parked in the cool shadows of his equipment shed. "Ten years ago we had a bumper crop, much more

than we could use, and Dad got on the phone to a mill up in Minnesota to try to sell our excess. 'No,' they said, 'we've got plenty of organic corn this year.' Dad was about to hang up when the man said, 'Wait a second. Are you Paul's Grains, the guys with the open-pollinated corn? We'll take all you've got!'" Steve laughs.

Corn can be pollinated on the wind from up to six miles away, which makes cross-contamination with nearby GMO corn an annual concern. To avoid this, Steve delays planting until several weeks after all of his neighbors are finished, creating his own isolated window of time for his corn to self-pollinate. Traveling from the tassel to the corn silk, each strand is a direct connection to an individual kernel. If no pollen reaches the silk, then no kernel will form.

Paul's saves its own seed each year, an old variety called Reid's Yellow Dent. "We use old-fashioned varieties for each

of our grains, so when you make oatmeal or cornbread with our flours, the flavor really comes through. The rye, for instance, Balboa Rye, it's smaller and full of beautiful colors, as opposed to the big gray rye that's commonly available." He crosses the dirt floor of the shed, toward a tarp-covered wagon. "Let me show you some of the corn we saved from last year, the Reid's Dent."

I'm tall, but not tall enough. The lip of the wagon is well over my head, so I stand on a tire as Steve pulls back a blue plastic tarp. Beneath, it's a landslide of kernels, a golden avalanche that glitters even in the shade of the building. Corn clicks through Steve's fingers as he scoops a bright handful, and he points out the elongated dent that gives the variety its name. Imagine, I think to myself, corn tasting like anything other than, well . . . *corn*. The idea that old varieties could possess more flavor had never occurred to me. Dusting off his palms, Steve leads me out into the fields.

It's my first time standing in an acre of buckwheat, and the view is serene, munificent. Neither a grass nor a legume, these plants have green heart-shaped leaves, crowned with white flowers reminiscent of baby's breath. Buckwheat is most closely related to rhubarb and sorrel, and until the early part of the twentieth century, more than a million acres of the crop were grown in the United States. By 1964, however, less than fifty thousand acres remained in production, a testament to the meteoric rise of corn and soybean production.

"Diversity plays a big role in our success," the farmer says, "not only for soil health, but to have different products to offer our customers. Oats, wheat, rye." He lowers himself to one

Did You Know?

Fifty percent of all conventional corn and soybeans grown in the United States are used for animal feed, and another 40 percent are used for ethanol production. The remaining percentages are used for high-fructose corn syrup, international food aid, and, lastly, for food ingredients.

knee, plucking the head from a nodding stem. "Buckwheat and spelt. You've got to work with the life of the soil—what God made—as well as work with the tractors, made by people. We try to find balance in everything we do."

Steve's son, Daniel, twenty-two, appears on a four-row cultivator, an old-fashioned device that mechanically scours weeds from rows of corn and soybeans. "Daniel's two hundred percent the farmer I am these days," Steve says affectionately. "We recently bought a second farm nearby, because Daniel wanted more land to work." Wiry and soft-spoken like his father, he has his mother Theresa's blue eyes, twinkling beneath the shade of his baseball cap. The family invites me into their store, where a self-service display offers their grains, flours, and free-range eggs for sale behind refrigerated glass.

"We recently stopped shipping out of state," Steve says, "because farm life is busy enough as it is. So you'd better take some cornmeal while you're here." Grateful, I reach for my wallet, but the farmer waives me off. "And take a bag of cucumbers," Theresa adds. "We've got far too many this year in the garden, even after pickling."

A sack of flour under one arm, vegetables under the other, I do my best to wave my good-byes without dropping the ingredients. The Midwest is famous for its warm hospitality, and Steve and Theresa don't disappoint. It's been a long time since I've had an experience like this, and as I drive away I can't shake the feeling that I've just visited a distant aunt and uncle.

At security in Des Moines, TSA makes me pull out my cucumbers. It's odd to see an armed guard, tattooed biceps bulging, scrutinizing produce as though it might be an exploding pickle, or a weapon of mass zucchini. Satisfied that it's a just

a garden-variety vegetable, I'm allowed to board with my cornmeal and cukes unconfiscated, gently placed into the overhead bin. If there had been an empty seat beside me, I might have even buckled them up for the flight.

Back at home, it's time for cornbread and salad. I follow the directions on the label, so simple even a non-foodie like myself couldn't screw it up. Flour, eggs, oil, and water. I'm out of honey, so I substitute a healthy dose of molasses to sweeten the deal. Into the oven for twenty-five minutes, as I slice the cucumbers and mix them with tomatoes that suddenly flourished in my garden while I was away.

Olive oil and balsamic on the salad, butter on the cornbread. The pat glides straight off the domed square, steam rising from the golden dough. The first bite melts on my tongue, buttery and sweet but substantial, the stoneground grains lending the noticeably hearty flavor that Steve had alluded to. Paired with crisp cucumber, bitter vinegar, and tangy tomato, it's little more than a modest summer meal. Yet, it's one of my finest in recent memory.

There's a song from the early eighties with the catchphrase, "I was country . . . when country wasn't cool." As a kid growing

up on my grandparents' West Virginia farm, I remember the chorus drifting from a cobwebby radio on the workbench, Barbara Mandrell's silver soprano contrasted with George Jones's creaky tenor, like a rusty ratchet tightening a shiny bolt.

Nine years old, dressed in my cousin's hand-me-downs and wearing an oversize red cap, I distinctly recall wondering, "Was country *ever* cool?" At night, I prayed that coolness might meander to our little corner of the Shenandoah Valley. I have a feeling Iowa farm kids hoped for a similar miracle.

But Paul's Grains, undoubtedly, was organic when organic wasn't cool—when organic farming was scarcely even a movement—and that's saying something. While big agriculture was blazing its trails, organic pioneers like Wayne steadfastly hoed their row. Fifty successful years later, it's important to know that a family farm can still take a stand in our modern world, remaining steadfast in its mission, and carve out an honest living. That is, and always has been, the true definition of country cool.

CITRUS BEETS

From Paul's Grains

Serves 2 to 4

2 tablespoons unsalted butter, melted

¼ cup honey

¼ cup fresh orange juice

2 tablespoons Paul's Grains flour* or other unbleached all-purpose flour

1 tablespoon fresh lemon juice

2 cups diced cooked beets

Melt the butter in a medium saucepan, then add the honey, orange juice, flour, and lemon juice. Cook over low heat until thickened, stirring frequently. Stir in the beets and cook until heated thoroughly. Serve while it's still warm.

*Available at paulsgrains.com

OAT BRAN CHOCOLATE CHIP COOKIES

From Paul's Grains

Makes about 4 dozen cookies

1. Preheat the oven to 350°F.

2. Whisk the brown sugar, oil, eggs and vanilla together in a large bowl. Add the remaining ingredients and mix well.

3. Form the dough into balls and place on a baking sheet. Bake for 10 to 12 minutes, until they begin to brown around the edges.

2 cups packed brown sugar

1 cup coconut oil

2 large eggs

1 teaspoon vanilla extract

2 cups Paul's Grains buckwheat flour or other buckwheat flour

2 cups Paul's Grains oat bran or other oat bran

1½ cups unsweetened shredded coconut

1 teaspoon baking soda

1 teaspoon baking powder

1 teaspoon salt

1 cup chocolate chips (or carob chips, if preferred)

1 cup chopped nuts, optional

RHUBARB BUCKWHEAT TORTE

From Heritage Hollow Farms

Inspired by Paul's Grains

Serves 8

CRUST

1 cup (2 sticks) melted unsalted butter

2 cups buckwheat flour

5 tablespoons sugar

FILLING

2 cups sugar

1 cup heavy cream

6 large egg yolks (save the egg whites in a separate bowl for the meringue)

¼ cup unbleached all-purpose flour

¼ teaspoon salt

5 cups chopped rhubarb

MERINGUE

6 large egg whites

¾ cup sugar

½ teaspoon salt

1 teaspoon vanilla extract

¼ teaspoon cream of tartar

1. Preheat the oven to 350°F.

2. To make the crust, blend together all the ingredients and press the mixture into a 13 x 9-inch baking dish, or 8 individual-size ramekins. Bake for 10 to 12 minutes.

3. To make the filling, beat the sugar, cream, egg yolks, flour, and salt in a large bowl until smooth. Add the rhubarb and stir to mix thoroughly. Remove the crust from the oven and pour in the filling. Bake for about 35 minutes, until the center is almost cooked through.

4. While the filling is in the oven, make the meringue: Using an electric mixer, beat the egg whites until foamy in a large bowl, gradually adding the sugar. Add the salt, vanilla, and cream of tartar and continue beating the whites until stiff peaks form. Drop the meringue onto the hot filling and bake for another 15 minutes. The torte is ready when the meringue peaks are lightly browned. Cool slightly before serving.

14

RED LAKE NATION FOODS

RED LAKE, MINNESOTA

Wild rice

////////////////////////////////////

Near Bemidji, Minnesota, the Mississippi River trickles from a single spring. In the distance the water sparkles beneath an evening sun, twinkling like a lullaby, singsong waves lapping a cadence against the reeded shores. Crossing the bridge on Highway 197, I pass Paul Bunyan and his ample ox, two-ton indulgences commissioned by the Rotary Club circa 1937. Over the years, tourists have flooded the small parking lot, snapping pictures before pouring back into their cars. One lake down, I tell myself, 9,999 to go. Even on dry land, our lives remain circumscribed by water.

A right turn, and due north to Red Lake. The largest body of water within the confines of Minnesota, this territory is the jurisdiction of Red Lake Nation, the ancestral birthright of the Ojibwa. Presently, the acreage covers an expanse roughly the size of Rhode Island. In the late 1800s, however, under the pretense of "relief and civilization of the Chippewa Indians," the federal government passed the Nelson Act, intended to transform the tribe's communally held lands into individual properties. In effect, the reservation would be carved into government-determined allotments—typically forty to one hundred acres—and then redistributed back to the tribal members. With the allotments adding up to significantly less than the original whole, newly available "surplus" land would afterward be put up for sale, most likely to white loggers eager to harvest the region's virgin timber. The Nelson Act violated decades-old treaties, and

was a thinly veiled ruse to carve the reservation into a checkerboard pattern, a classic divide-and-conquer strategy. It was passed by Congress on January 14, 1889.

Ojibwa tribal elders didn't go for it. Recognizing that their people would never be fairly compensated, the council refused to cede its core holdings—specifically the vast area surrounding upper and lower Red Lake. While some portions of the territory were eventually ceded and allotted, the heart of the region was kept intact, an area of nearly one thousand square miles. Red Lake is one of only a handful of reservations in the country that stood up to the Nelson Act, and the tribe is now recognized by the federal government as having full sovereignty over the area.

This is where I'm headed today. Miles fly past, bordered by quaking aspen and paper birch, glimpses of silvery water through the picketing trees. A gas station emerges from the wilderness, and I pull off the highway to meet Harvey Roy, a tribal member and head of Red Lake Nation Foods, home to six hundred acres of wild rice. I follow Harvey up the road to Redby, a small town along the water's edge.

As a sovereign nation, permission to visit must be granted. Tribal chairman Darrel Seki greets us in the conference room, sporting lavender sunglasses and a black ponytail flumed between his shoulders. Although Seki is welcoming and quick with a laugh, there's a tacit understanding that my motivations are being weighed, my responses to his questions thoughtfully vetted. In the end, our mutual bond with agriculture carries the day. The chairman gives his blessing—as well a few good-natured Forrest Gump references—and I'm welcomed as an official guest. To quote Tom Hanks, that's all I have to say about that.

Harvey introduces me to Joel Rohde, a former biologist for the Department of Natural Resources who is now a full-time farmer. Soft-spoken and genial, Joel was hired by Red Lake in 1997 to help create a commercially viable wild-rice farm, improving a tract of land purchased by the tribe when it became available adjacent to the reservation. The farming was rough from day one.

"That first year, we were so optimistic. We got the seed planted, and the rice was coming up better than we ever imagined. Then"—Joel's face darkens—"a tornado came through. The farmer next door had just been making hay, and it picked up all his bales and tossed them into our paddies. I'm talking half-ton round bales, like they were dropped straight out of the sky. Between that and the wind, it flattened the crop, made it impossible to harvest. We almost thought we'd have to give up after that first year.

But we planted again and had a great season, so we've been doing it ever since." He waves us on. "Let's drive out to the farm, and I'll show you the rice."

Harvey and I follow Joel's pickup, a hunter-green Dodge with a northern pike airbrushed onto the tailgate. It's a long trip, the better part of an hour, and we pass fewer than a dozen cars as we navigate the remote Minnesota straightaways. Endless lakes, endless trees—it's hard to imagine how anyone could farm here with arable ground so scarce. All at once the dense tree line breaks and the land is flooded in light, showcasing open fields of alfalfa, potatoes, oats. We've entered farm country. Joel's truck bears right onto a side road, white gravel crunching beneath our tires, plumes of pale dust billowing above the stubbled hayfields of summer.

Though we're miles from the closest town, the streets out here are still clearly marked. The farm, I can't help but notice, is on the corner of 580th and 139th, two green street signs crossed on the perpendicular, X marking the spot. Harvey had warned me to fill my tank before we left, and I was now appreciative for the advice; it had been an hour since I'd seen a gas station, a half hour since I'd had a cell signal. After a final mile of driving, we park in a modest barnyard, two cavernous steel buildings sheltering tools and tractors. Farm manager John Sandland, sixty-three, greets us with a curt wave, a tanned face beneath cropped white hair, eyes crinkled from a lifetime of working in the sun. Hopping into his pickup truck, we drive out to see the rice paddies.

The fields resemble nothing so much as enormous, shallow bathtubs, perfectly flat across the bottom, then sloping into four-foot-tall earthen berms along the edges. Out-

side the levee, a perimeter dike surrounds the paddy like a moat, knee-deep with water pumped from nearby Clearwater River. John steps down into a paddy, the black, spongy soil seeping water with each step, and wades waist-deep into a hundred acres of wild rice.

At first glance the paddy could be mistaken for an ordinary hayfield: elegant grass stems bowing to the breeze, a green drop cloth beneath a mural of azure sky. But closer inspection reveals a cascade of ripening seed, dark grains suspended above purple flowers. John bends a seed head into his calloused palm, studying the crop.

"It's been a late spring, so the seed heads are just coming on now, the flowers barely out." Cupped in his hand, he nudges the rice with a fingertip, snapping off a single hull. "This is an improved variety, developed by the University of Minnesota. See, hundreds of years ago, when Native Americans used to

harvest rice in canoes, the seed was so fragile it would shatter when it landed, breaking into pieces. But this variety has been crossed twelve times, wild plants bred again and again to improve kernel strength. Now, we only lose about five percent to shattering. It's a huge improvement."

The result? A variety that meets their needs without the patent restrictions of a GMO product, allowing the farmers to retain their own seeds. "Yeah," John acknowledges. "We save our own seed each year and plant it again in the fall, usually around September or October, right after the late-summer harvest."

The farmer lowers himself to one knee, probing the marshy ground with an index finger. "Even on the very edge of the paddy, you can see how saturated the ground is. But wild rice is unique, because unlike other plants, it doesn't germinate just because of moisture. It has to go through a cool period first, then make up its mind the following year whether or not it'll grow. Sometimes it takes a year or two to decide, and we don't get a crop." He chuckles humorlessly. "As you can imagine, that comes with its own challenges."

Corralling a waving grass stem, he strips a row of rice through his fingers, holding a single seed against the sky. "Here, look at this." With sunlight filtering through, the hull has become translucent green, like a tiny neon glow stick.

"Right now, this is just an empty shell, more or less a tube. But in the next month, it'll fill with seed from the inside out. It's really neat to observe." A mysterious smile forms on his lips. "Don't ask me how or why it works like that," he continues, anticipating my next question. "Nobody knows. It just does."

Only a short distance into the paddy, we're forced to stop. Deeper water now pools along the root tops. John drops to his haunches, scooping a handful of spongy earth.

"The trick is keeping the water levels just right," he explains. "Too deep, the seed can't get enough sunlight to grow. But if it's too shallow, it doesn't provide the stem with enough support." He squeezes the soil in his fist, and black water trickles between his knuckles. "It's always a balancing act," he says, allowing the earth to slip from his hands, "a tightrope, finding our way to a successful harvest each year."

Impossible to tell by eye, each field tips on a very gradual slope, roughly ten feet over four miles. In the spring, water is pumped into the paddies, then drained by gravity through metal floodgates in the fall. The draining takes about six weeks. Not because it can't be done faster, John explains. Instead, time is needed for the grass to adapt and strengthen in the absence of water, otherwise stalks would collapse onto the ground, rendering the crop unharvestable.

Mimicking Native American techniques, early commercial rice farmers used boats to harvest the fall crop, knocking seed onto the floor as they passed back and forth through flooded patties. These days, however, once the ground is dry enough, wooden-tracked combines enter the paddies, combing the grass with rotary tines that sweep the seeds into a catchment chamber. Once gleaned, the rice is then trucked to a local mill to be dried, reducing moisture to the point where it eventually becomes shelf-stable. Later that afternoon, back at the warehouse, Joel and Harvey cut the strings on a bulging white tote bag, fabric stretched to bursting with a thousand pounds of delicate black grains.

Did You Know?

Compared to white rice, wild rice has more protein, fiber, vitamin B6, and riboflavin, as well as zinc and magnesium, with fewer overall calories. Additionally, the protein found in wild rice carries higher levels of lysine and methionine, important amino acids for balanced nutrition.

Catching the light, the seed gleams as brightly as bronze. I cup two handfuls, holding it to my nose and inhaling deeply. Woody and warm, the aroma carries a breath of summer wind across lake water, with lingering notes of birch and red pine. It's a flavor that belongs to Minnesota, to her lakes, to her people.

Harvey leads me from the warehouse, and a short time later we're standing on the banks of Lower Red Lake. Birdsong fills the air, yellow warblers and rose-breasted grosbeaks banking beneath colossal midsummer clouds. Wildflowers sway at our knees, crown vetch and heliotrope, belted clover drowsing in the afternoon sun. It's a quintessential July day, one you'd like to bottle and open on a frozen Midwestern night. Harvey gestures beyond the gentle waves, pointing to an invisible destination in the northern distance.

"Out on the peninsula, separating the lakes, that's Ponemah. It's the most traditional village in our nation. We have our annual Labor Day powwow there, four days long. It's huge, open to the public. People come from all over the country to see it."

He pauses, silently studying the waves. "We call ourselves the *anishinaabe*," he volunteers at last, "'the original people.' As I get older, I'm trying to learn more about my ancestry, more of my language. Two of my uncles are farmers, and if that's a direction I decide to go, then the tribe will provide the land." He nods, considering. "There's a lot of opportunities up here, really."

Minnesota is a Lakota phrase combining *minni*—"water"— with *sotah*—"sky-tinted." In a land of ten thousand lakes, rice is nature's link between water and heavens, earthly abundance reaching skyward in the wooded, eddying backwaters. The wind moves, and I imagine the sound of rice falling against birch bark, clicks like raindrops on a hot summer day. Echoes, and a solitary canoe rippling through dark water. A paddle rises, flashes, stirring the silence. Along the sloping banks, generations of harvests await.

WILD RICE PANCAKES
WITH APPLE TOPPING

From Red Lake Nation Foods

Makes sixteen 4-inch pancakes and 2 cups of apple topping

One 1½-pound package
  Red Lake Nation Wild Rice
  Pancake Mix,* or other wild
  rice pancake mix

3 medium apples, peeled,
  cored, and sliced

2 tablespoons apple cider

2 teaspoons fresh lemon juice,
  or to taste

½ cup pure maple syrup

2 tablespoons unsalted butter

1. Prepare the pancakes according to the package directions. Keep them warm in an oven on the lowest setting while you make the apple topping.

2. Place the apples, cider, and lemon juice in a medium saucepan over low heat and cook until the apples are semi-translucent and bubbling.

3. Add the maple syrup and heat through. Remove from the heat and add the butter.

4. Pour the warm apple topping over the pancakes and enjoy.

*Available at redlakenationfoods.com

WILD RICE MEATBALLS

From Red Lake Nation Foods

Makes about 9 dozen appetizer-size meatballs

MEATBALLS

2 pounds grass-fed ground
  beef

1 pound ground pork (forest-
  raised, if possible)

1¾ cups cooked Red Lake
  Nation wild rice (any
  variety)*, or other wild rice

1¼ cups old-fashioned oats

½ cup chopped onion

2 large eggs

SAUCE

½ cup heavy cream

2 teaspoons chili powder

2 teaspoons salt

¾ teaspoon garlic powder

½ teaspoon freshly ground
  black pepper

1. Preheat the oven to 350°F.

2. For the meatballs, mix all the ingredients together in a large bowl. Using your hands, shape into 1-inch balls. Arrange in a large baking pan in a single layer.

3. For the sauce, whisk the ingredients together and pour over the meatballs. Cover with aluminum foil and bake for 1 hour.

*Available at redlakenationfoods.com

15

RONNYBROOK FARM DAIRY

ANCRAMDALE, HUDSON VALLEY, NEW YORK

Cow milk, yogurt, butter, and ice cream

It's a beautiful morning in mid-June, and I'm eating vanilla ice cream with a raucous group of kindergartners, schoolchildren on their annual farm tour. Beyond our picnic table, the Catskill Mountains provide a green backdrop for a herd of black-and-white Holsteins, a hundred cattle grazing on lush pasture between their twice-daily milkings. Across from me, farmer emeritus Ronny Osofsky, seventy-three, leans toward the five-year-old seated beside him, adopting a conspiratorial tone typically reserved for old poker buddies.

"So how's that vanilla?" he asks. "Any good?"

The boy's blond, crew-cut head bobs up and down enthusiastically. "Yeah. It's good!"

Next, the old farmer inclines his chin toward a half-emptied bottle. "And the chocolate milk," he inquires. "How was that?"

"Good!"

Ronny nods pensively, making every appearance of ruminating over the review. He smooths his disheveled beard, closing heavy eyelids as he composes his thoughts. "Let me ask you, last questions: What about the coconut yogurt? And the strawberry smoothie? And the cream-line milk?"

"Good. Good! GOOD!" The responses crescendo into an exasperated headshake, the delighted kindergartner wondering what this irrepressible

farmer could possibly be up to. After all, when you're five years old, what could be better than ice cream before lunch?

Beyond a doubt, things seem to be good at Ronnybrook. Good, and busy. After starting with what seemed like a basic concept in 1991—to bottle their whole milk and sell it to customers in New York City—the eight-hundred-acre farm now produces so many variations of milk, yogurt, and butter that they occasionally lose track of precisely how many. "It depends on the season," Ronny concedes, "and that doesn't just apply to us. For example, our drinkable yogurts are the most popular thing we make, and we source most of the fruit—coconut and mango excepted—from other local farms. So it's not unusual for us to run out from time to time."

The Osofskys' dairy is a bona fide throwback, an operation that milks, bottles, and delivers its own products. The wardrobe has undoubtedly changed—no white milkman caps to be found on the premises—but the spirit of service remains vitally alive, right down to the reusable glass bottles. Per traditions dating back to the old country, when Ronny's parents purchased the land in 1941, they named the farm after their first son. But younger brother, Rick, seventy, and their respective children, all play crucial roles: from milking to management to maintenance, to waking at three in the morning to drive to market.

"Yeah, I just wrapped up a weekend of farmers' markets," says Ronny's nephew Peter, thirty-nine, "and made it home in time to celebrate my daughter's birthday on Sunday night. Today—Monday—this is my day off." He smiles wearily, but his eyes are bright with good humor. "And look, I'm running to get parts for a broke-down tractor. But don't let me slow you down. You should go see the milking barn."

Directly across the road, the barn is painted periwinkle blue and capped with a peaked tin roof. Replete with shadows, its floor polished smooth by generations of hooves and boot heels, the building carries the sanctified air of a cathedral, consecrated and cool with a Hudson breeze pushing through the eaves. I ask Ronny the age of the building, and he sighs with the weight of decades. "It's old," he replies matter-of-factly. "Older even than me."

The cows proceed in single file, led to their stanchions as if by rote. Above each dais, a name: Mabel. Cora. Norma. It's as if the monikers have been yanked straight out of a *Laverne and Shirley* episode, Milwaukee circa 1957. The Holsteins don't care a whit, munching tranquilly on fermented silage, belching their cud, moon-eyed and docile as the farmhands go about their milking. A short time later the ladies will be back on pasture, enjoying an afternoon graze.

"The difference between a milking barn and a milking parlor?" Ronny volunteers. "In a parlor, the cows come to the milker. In a barn, we roll the milker to them. We're able to milk six at a time; takes about an hour and a half, two hours. Four in the morning, then again at five P.M."

Ronny's Farm Humor

"My brother, Rick, is the CEO. That is, he would be if we gave titles. Who needs titles on a family farm? Everybody knows who everybody is."

The milk is soon pasteurized, a process of quickly raising then lowering the temperature in a twenty-second flash. "We do the gentlest pasteurization allowed," Ronny explains, "otherwise, the milk goes totally sterile, lifeless. No flavor whatsoever. This ultra-pasteurization nowadays, where they heat it so high the shelf life lasts forever?" He rolls his eyes. "What's the point of that? It just tastes like water."

I consider the simple wisdom of his logic. Why drink milk that doesn't taste like milk? There's plenty of Dasani and Aquafina on the market already. "Take our yogurt, for example," he continues. "It's tart. Less time in the heat leaves it with a touch of acidity, like it is in Europe. Our drinkable yogurt has ten live cultures in it; most others on the market only have four." He winks. "We wanted to put that on our label, but a big company had beat us to it and trademarked it."

Just outside the barn, a sedan goes whizzing past. A public road divides the dairy in two, making it impossible to pipe milk straight from the barn to the receiving tanks. Instead, it must be trundled across by truck, where it's then poured into stainless receiving tanks.

"We're building a new pasteurizer, one that'll handle more volume. Forty thousand dollars in parts, another forty thousand in labor. Currently, we process three hundred gallons an hour, but this new machine will get us up to twelve hundred. That's huge, because we've got guys ready to bottle, but right now they've gotta wait." The old farmer guffaws. "I guess you could say we've got a bottling bottleneck."

The new pasteurizer is a work in progress. Parts and pipes are scattered across the room, soldering rods and a welding mask discarded beside an intricate blueprint, all spread across a wooden workbench. The room carries the look of an Erector set dumped on the carpet on Christmas morning, a magnificent metal jumble in search of a qualified engineer. The engineer, as it turns out, is named Bob.

Did You Know?

Ronnybrook's cows produce between seventy-six and seventy-eight pounds of milk, or roughly ten gallons, every day.

Bob explains the process, gesturing with a length of stainless steel. "Raw milk is pumped through the balance tank, then sent up the pipes. The water goes up one side at one hundred and forty degrees Fahrenheit, and the milk comes down the other. We hold it there for twenty seconds, and it kills off bacteria. Then, it's sent through the separator, which skims off the fat. We send the skim to a holding tank and reblend it with cream farther down the line, depending on the end product." Bob pauses, arms folded over his chest. "How'd I do, Ron? Did I explain it okay?"

"You did a nice job there, Bob."

"Good. Then next time, *I* get to take the tour."

In the clanking bottling room, filled with white noise and white milk, empty glass pints clink as they are conveyed, filled, and instantly capped. Next door, the processing facility is a cavernous room mosaicked with chocolate- and caramel-

colored tiles, light filtering through the translucent windows and brightening the corners of stainless steel machines. Here, yogurt is blended, fruit is pared, and butter is churned. An avalanche of empty maple syrup jugs, used to flavor the yogurt, await recycling nearby.

It's just past noon, and workers doff hairnets as they head to lunch. Ronny chats cordially with his chief butter-maker, Edna, an employee of fourteen years, cracking a joke just beyond my earshot. Without warning she throws an arm around the farmer's shoulders, giving him a warm pat on the chest.

"What a great guy to work for," she says earnestly, her face illuminating the room. "And you can write that in your book! I love this old man."

He shrugs abashedly as she exits, clearly embarrassed by the attention. "You know," he volunteers, "if you had asked me how many people work here, my first instinct might be to say ten, maybe fifteen. But that's living in the past, back when Edna first started. We've got *fifty* employees now." The old farmer gestures broadly, marveling. "Things just keep growing."

Outside, it's a perfect summer afternoon in Upstate New York. Taking our time, talking farming all the way, Ronny leads me across the cow pasture and up a steep hill overlooking the dairy. The view is expansive, the Hudson Valley stretched before us like a rumpled quilt, a patchwork of greens and yellows stitched with locust fence posts. To the east, hazy through the June sunshine, the Berkshires and neighboring Massachusetts; to the west, the Catskills and the state capital of Albany.

"It's funny, you know? We just signed up with a place called Berkshire Farms Market. They've put in a store at Logan airport in Boston, only carrying local products." He removes his crumpled baseball cap, tapping it against his knee thoughtfully. "I mean, we're not even in the Berkshires." He laughs. "And we're not in the Catskills, either. We're just where we are. Right here." His eyes sparkle with mirth as he replaces his hat. "People want us to be everywhere. But there's only so much we can do, so much any one farm can do." He looks eastward. "I'll be curious, though, to see how yogurt sells at an airport. Let me know if you stumble across it."

Ronny's Farm Humor

"There's no such thing as an expert. You know what an expert is? It's a 'spert' who didn't make it."

In rare Hollywood fashion, it all goes down as if scripted. Berkshire Farms Market, as blind luck would have it, is directly adjacent to my gate, B22. I'm in line to purchase my Ronnybrook smoothie, the final peach in a sold-out rack. Just in front of me, a smartly dressed woman in a black business suit studies the menu.

"So," she asks. "All of these products honestly come from local farms?"

The cashier, a young woman dressed in a logoed polo and matching hat, looks thoroughly confounded by the question.

"Umm . . . from what?"

"From local farms." The woman motions to the sign on the wall. "That's what it says, that everything here is locally sourced."

The cashier turns hesitatingly toward a coworker, who raises her palms in self-defense. "Don't look at me," her expression seems to say. "I don't speak Farm."

"Like," the cashier replies at last, "like, I've literally got no idea. Let me go get my manager . . ."

"Actually," I interrupt, naturally shy, but summoning the courage to pull a deus ex machina. "I . . . feel oddly qualified to answer that question."

In short order, I detail my visit to Ancramdale, my conversations with Ronny, as well as the inherent irony of the entire situation. Meanwhile, the two cashiers have slowly backed away, adopting expressions typically reserved for encounters with doomsday street preachers. To my surprise, business-suit lady is only slightly less skeptical.

"So you were just out at the farm this morning? Really." She says this with unexpected intensity, like a lawyer cross-questioning a witness. Defensively, I feel the urge to reach for a badge that doesn't exist, something that says, "Relax, I'm a farmer!" with a smiley face in a straw hat.

All at once, she softens. "I'm sorry," she says. "It's nothing personal. It's just, you know," she pauses, searching for the right words. "Sometimes it's hard to believe all this food is coming from family farms. Part of me thinks it's all a big scam, cooked up by companies to make a buck." She purses her lips into a thin frown. "It's a shame, isn't it? To become so cynical about something like local food."

Not at all, I tell her, more empathetic than she could possibly know. I think back to Ronny, a happy old farmer eating ice cream with kids on a summer morning, and ask myself: Who would be gullible enough to believe such a fairy tale? But I've got little time to reflect. Moments later my flight is boarding, and I find myself lost in the crush of mid-Atlantic commuters and carry-ons. The line shifts immutably forward, one pinging barcode scan at a time.

Before I board, however, I finish that peach smoothie. And you know what I think? The kindergartner had it right all along. It was *good*.

EGGNOG FRENCH TOAST

WITH MAPLE WHIPPED CREAM AND CINNAMON BUTTER

From Ronnybrook Farm Dairy

Serves 3 to 5

1. Preheat the oven to 250°F.

2. Whisk the eggs, eggnog, and salt in a large, shallow bowl or dish. Soak the bread slices in the egg mixture for about 3 minutes, turning once. You may not be able to fit all the bread in the dish at once, so do it in batches if necessary, transferring the already-soaked pieces to another dish until ready to cook.

3. Heat the oil and cinnamon butter in a large skillet over medium heat. Add a few slices of soaked bread and cook for 2 to 3 minutes on each side, until browned. Transfer the cooked French toast to a baking sheet and place the sheet in the oven. Cook the remaining bread slices, adding more cinnamon butter and oil as needed.

4. Serve the hot French toast with a dollop of maple whipped cream and cinnamon butter. Garnish with fresh berries if desired.

6 extra-large eggs

1½ cups Ronnybrook Eggnog, if available in your area, or other eggnog

½ teaspoon kosher salt

1 large loaf challah or brioche, sliced ¾ inch thick

1 tablespoon coconut oil + extra as needed

1 tablespoon Cinnamon Butter + extra as needed (recipe follows, or use Ronnybrook Cinnamon Butter, if available)

Maple Whipped Cream (recipe follows)

Fresh berries, optional

MAPLE WHIPPED CREAM

Place a large metal bowl in the refrigerator to chill, at least 30 minutes. Beat the heavy cream and maple syrup together in the chilled bowl, using an electric mixer or a whisk, until the mixture stiffens.

1 cup heavy cream

1 tablespoon pure maple syrup, or to taste

CINNAMON BUTTER

4 tablespoons (½ stick) unsalted butter, at room temperature

2 teaspoons cinnamon, or to taste

2 teaspoons sugar, or to taste

Whip the butter, cinnamon, and sugar in a medium bowl, using a whisk or (for a smoother, creamier texture) an electric mixer.

FRESH RICOTTA

From John MacPherson at Foster Harris House

Inspired by Ronnybrook Farm Dairy

Serves 4 to 6

8 cups whole milk

4 cups heavy cream

2 teaspoons kosher salt

6 tablespoons high-quality white wine vinegar

1. Place a large fine-mesh strainer over a deep bowl and line it with cheesecloth. Set aside.

2. Pour the milk and cream into a large stainless steel saucepan. Stir in the salt. Bring to a full boil over medium heat, stirring occasionally. Turn off the heat and stir in the vinegar. Let the mixture stand for 1 minute until it curdles. It will separate into thick parts (the curds) and milky parts (the whey).

3. Pour the mixture through the cheesecloth into the strainer and allow it to drain into the bowl for 20 to 25 minutes at room temperature, occasionally discarding the liquid that collects in the bowl. The longer you let the mixture drain, the thicker the ricotta.

4. Transfer the ricotta to a bowl, discarding the cheesecloth and any remaining whey. Use immediately or cover with plastic wrap and refrigerate. The ricotta will keep refrigerated for 4 to 5 days.

DULCE DE LECHE

From Heritage Hollow Farms

Inspired by Ronnybrook Farm Dairy

Makes about 1¼ cups

1. Combine the milk, sugar, and sea salt in a medium saucepan. Whisk lightly and bring to a simmer over medium heat.

2. Remove the pan from the heat and whisk in the baking soda. Return to medium heat and simmer for about 1 hour, occasionally skimming off the foam that develops and stirring gently. Watch closely as it reduces and turns golden brown, cooking for another 1 to 1½ hours; lower the heat as needed to ensure it doesn't burn.

3. Strain through a fine-mesh strainer. Serve immediately or store in a sealed container in the refrigerator for up to a month (although it will almost certainly be devoured within the first week).

4 cups whole milk
1½ cups sugar
¼ teaspoon sea salt
¾ teaspoon baking soda

16

JOSEPH FIELDS FARM

CHARLESTON, SOUTH CAROLINA

Organic produce

It's late spring, and the sun is in full glory above Johns Island, just south of Charleston. Joseph Fields stoops over his strawberry patch, his forehead brightly beaded with sweat, hands working decisively. The bucket quickly fills with berries.

"How many days till those go to market?" I ask, noticing the fruit hasn't fully ripened yet.

"Days?" Joseph repeats, his expression askance. He chuckles. "There's no *days*." The farmer softly drops a pink berry into the white bucket. "To-*day*," he enunciates. "That's Gullah talk. Picked fresh. In heat like this, the fruit'll ripen for tonight's dessert."

Something is always in season at Joseph Fields' farm. Coastal winds push across Charleston Harbor, supplying Gulf Stream warmth to this corner of the South. "We've got kale, collards, onions. Broccoli, lettuce. Okra and toma-toes." He pivots as he speaks, taking in the full circumference of his fifty-acre farm. "Cantaloupe, watermelon, potatoes, beans. Whatever we want to grow, we can grow it here. We even have a banana tree."

Johns Island is one of the largest islands on the East Coast, and the sea air is perfumed with palmetto and pine. The sandy soil is the color of chocolate milk, rich with loam and sprinkled with tiny white seashells. The farmer stands with his hands on his hips, observing his crew in the distance, workers in

wide-brimmed hats harvesting vegetables for this afternoon's farmers' market.

"When I went organic," Joseph recalls, "I took it one acre at a time. Slow, being patient, gaining experience. I've been farming most of my life, and you don't just change everything overnight." He smooths the gray wisp of soul patch adorning his chin, considering. "You want to go for a walk, see my farm? Okay, then. Let's go."

Joseph farms land that's been handed down for three consecutive generations. At age sixty-five the farmer has no trouble keeping a steady pace, his stories and thoughts free-flowing as he leads the way. I hurry to catch up as he strides past aging planters, sprayers, and decrepit tractors rusting into retirement.

"The land has been certified organic for about five years now, and a lot of this stuff," he says, nodding to the defunct machinery, "I just don't need it anymore. Why did we go organic? Because the customers asked for it, and I like it, too. I'm the youngest of eight kids, but my sister, she still farms six acres near here. Now she's going organic as well." He smiles, nodding. "I'm helping her with the transition."

This region of South Carolina is steeped in agricultural heritage, with farming predating the Revolutionary War by more than a century. Generations of indigo plantations were followed by cotton, then succeeded by sweet potatoes, tomatoes, and cucumbers. However, a cultural shift has come to this corner of South Carolina. The local population recently soared,

Joseph's Farming Wisdom

"People come to the farmers' markets because they want to see the hands that grew their food. This is hands-on food! You can't get that at a grocery store."

doubling between 2000 and 2010, and these days housing developments outstrip farm production. A mile or so from Joseph's farm, a billboard announces the arrival of a Harris Teeter grocery store, set to compete with a Food Lion supermarket directly across the street. The farmer smiles knowingly.

"Yeah, I'll be selling to that new store. We've already been talking." He squints against the bright sun, pointing to the heavily trafficked highway running near his farm. "Look. You see all these new cars, all these people? This is no hobby. It's a business. Things are changing around here, and you've got to be smart."

The average age of the American farmer is fifty-nine. In a profession where an entire generation is approaching retirement, it's remarkable to find Joseph so deeply in tune with his customers. "The new thing?" he volunteers. "Making juices. People are buying bunches of kale, juicing it, or making kale chips, things like that." The farmer shrugs modestly. "Hey, when the vegetables are ready, you've got to sell them, right? Food is for people to eat, not look at. Farmers' markets. Restaurants. Wholesale. I do all of it."

Rows of sweet peas, eggplants, and seedling tomatoes extend for a quarter mile, young plants that are just taking root. It's been an extraordinarily cold winter, and even with the steady warm air that's now pushing along the coast, spring remains a month behind. Still, as every gardener knows, weeds know no season. Joseph pauses near the end of a long row.

"You know what this is?" He points to a knee-high plant, thick with dark green leaves. "Most people think this is a weed, and they rip it out, wasting it. But this is callaloo." The farmer tears off a leaf and pops it into his mouth. "You cook it up, mix it

with your collard greens," he explains, chewing. "People have been eating this for hundreds of years. Caribbean people, you know? It's good for you."

Following his lead, I pull a spear-tipped leaf from the stalk. The flavor is mild, neither as astringent as spinach nor as bitter as chard, with a lingering flavor of parsley in the aftertaste. I take a second helping, snacking as he speaks.

"In the winter, it's cabbage, mustard, turnips. *Greens*," he says enthusiastically, managing to stretch the word into two syllables. "I grow what I like to eat, my favorites, that's the best part of farming how I do."

Did You Know?

Regular consumption of cruciferous vegetables (collards, kale, broccoli, radishes, etc.) has been strongly linked to cancer prevention, and is also known to help reverse type 2 diabetes.

A third-generation farmer, Joseph grew up as a farm kid in the 1950s, following in his family's footsteps. His father taught him how to grow vegetables, a legacy he hoped one day to pass on to his own son. But it wasn't to be.

"My son, when he was little, I had to give him one of my kidneys." The old farmer somberly pats his side, nodding meaningfully. "That's the reason he couldn't be a farmer like me; he had to get a job with the Department of Transportation. Health insurance, right? Hard to pay for insurance just from farming. But he helps me every weekend at the markets." He brightens at the thought. "Come on, let's keep moving. I'll show you where I grew up."

Waiting for a break in the traffic, we cross the busy two-lane highway. Spanish moss hangs in soft, gray strands from the live oaks, gently swaying beneath shadowed limbs. Across the road, a group of locals stand talking in a dusty parking lot, old pickup trucks parked haphazardly, their conversation at a low hum. Late-model sedans buzz past, but these men seem to be in no hurry. The farmer waves to them, then gestures to a modest brick house with a grassy backyard.

"This is where I was raised, starting back in 1949. We kept chickens, had a place where we'd scald hogs in the fall. We had one tractor, one horse. When winter came, we cured sweet potatoes and sold them to folks from the front porch."

He stands, hands in pockets, surveying the neatly mowed yard. "In the back, we had a shed where we'd make cane syrup. Boil the sugar cane, you understand. It's making a big comeback now, people using it to make their own sugar, or just to chew on. But when I was a kid, man! That was some hard work. It's funny to see how things come around again."

Beneath an archway of pines, boughs laced over our heads, birds trill a chorus of spring nesting songs. Another vast field opens before us, and Joseph kneels beside a raised bed, covered in thick black plastic for a hundred yards or more. Every few feet, through a puncture in the plastic, a delicate sprout is growing, spreading green leaves beneath the warm Carolina sunshine.

"You like peanuts, yeah? We plant them when it's cool, then they're ready in June. Each plant yields about a pound, maybe a pound and a half. A lot of people don't know it, but peanuts are a legume, and they grow in their shells underground. We harvest these with a potato machine, knock the dirt off, then they're ready to boil or roast. Boiled peanuts, that's a Southern specialty."

A newbie to the boiled-peanut scene, I couldn't help but notice their popularity on my drive in; there seemed to be a billboard for stewed goobers on the outskirts of every small town I passed. Earlier that morning I had succumbed, stopping at a ramshackle roadside stand with a hand-painted sign for HOT BOILED PEANUTS steeped in a large black kettle. Salty steam curled from the cup as the attendant ladled my serving. To my surprise, I discovered that the shells were left on.

Did You Know?

Although the names are commonly interchanged, yams and sweet potatoes are different vegetables, each coming from a separate plant family. Yams originated in Africa and Asia, and sweet potatoes from Central and South America. As a rule of thumb, sweet potatoes are smooth-skinned and naturally sweet, while yams are rough-skinned and starchy.

"Yeah, there's two kinds," the man explained, "soft shell and hard. Just pop them in your mouth—shell and all—and suck out the juice. If the shell's soft, you eat the whole thing. If not, you just eat the peanuts and spit out the hull."

I held a steaming shell between my thumb and index finger as if it was a baby carrot, tentatively biting it in half. In a blink, hot liquid jetted from the opposite end like a squirt gun, thick brine dripping down the clean glass of the deli display.

"Ha! That's what everyone does the first time." The clerk politely brushed away my apology as he wiped down the glass with a rag. "You've got to put the whole thing in your mouth. Crunch it up."

This time, I followed orders. I popped a peanut, breaking the shell with my jaw. The warm, soupy brine was nothing short of delicious, a flavor most closely resembling russet potato skins. The nuts themselves were an earthier version of

edamame, a subsoil reflection of their aboveground soybean cousins. I carried the cup to my car, enjoying another, then another, spitting hulls from the window like a baseball player with sunflower seeds. Before I knew it, I had found the bottom of the cup.

Beyond the rows of young peanuts, Joseph points to where his grandparents once worked, the original fields now thickly wooded in trees. "You've got to plant in succession," he says, explaining the purpose behind the woodland regrowth. "Let things rest, rotate. Of course, the deer take their fair share, too, but that's just part of farming." Rounding a turn, he comes to a halt. "And here's another part."

He gestures to a row of greenhouses, where strips of torn plastic flutter listlessly in the breeze. The exposed metal bars, intended to be covered in translucent plastic, now resemble a shipwreck, bleached timbers cast helplessly upon the shore.

"High winds," he says by way of explanation. The destruction is a reminder that this is hurricane country, and strong coastal winds are the norm. "Those hoop houses are used to train our apprentices, young people who come here to learn." He nudges a remnant of windblown plastic, now tattered and useless, with his boot, "There's more to learn about farming than just seeds and watering cans. The apprentices find that out when they come here."

Past the barren framework, rows of sweet potatoes guide us back to the main driveway. "I like working with young people, though," Joseph continues, "even little kids. Each year, I plant a garden at a day-care center in the city. Afterwards, when the plants are growing, we go out to the garden. I ask the kids, 'Where does food come from?' They all speak at once. 'The store,' they say. 'Well, how does it get to the store?' I ask them. And you know what? They don't know."

A pickup truck loaded with produce rolls down the driveway, headed to the Mount Vernon farmers' market just north of Charleston. The driver, Mike, has been working for Joseph for five years. He leans out of his window to speak to us.

"Yeah, organics has come slowly to the South, but now Charleston has become a real foodie town. As someone who's lived here a long time, it's cool to see. But even for me—and I'll be fifty this year—I never thought about where my food comes from. For the first couple of years, this was just a delivery job, and it never even crossed my mind. Then one day, I was out in the field, helping load strawberries, eating a few as I went.

"And that's when it hit me: 'Hey, I don't have to wash the pesticide off of this. I can just eat it right off the stem.'"

Did You Know?

Strawberries are a truly unique fruit. Not only are they always the first berries of spring, they are the only fruit that exposes their seeds on the outside of their skin. Never noticed? Take a look!

Mike thumbs toward the old farmer, who nods wordlessly in response. "Pretty basic concept, right? But I'd never taken a second to think about it. Ever since then, I've paid attention to what I eat, how it's grown."

Over the years, Joseph Fields has probably heard dozens of stories like this. As Mike drives away Joseph stands with arms crossed, studying the cloud of dust.

"My grandson, he wants to be a farmer like me." He pauses, smiling as only a proud grandfather can. "He's in the fourth grade, just ten years old. Looks like I'm gonna have to farm a little longer, keep the place up until he's ready."

Passing his coop, Joseph clucks happily at his chickens, and playfully calls to the ponies that he shelters nearby, for weekend visits with his grandchildren. At the packing sheds, a large crew is busily washing vegetables, sorting crates, loading more market trucks. After waving a round of hellos, Joseph sits heavily on a lowered tailgate, the first indication he's ready to rest for more than a moment. The farmer smiles briefly, then knits his brow in thought.

"Time waits for no one, my friend. *No one.*" He shifts on the tailgate, and spreads his arms wide. "But these days, everybody's moving here, building houses. The land prices are so high. What's gonna happen? Who's gonna farm?"

I want to respond, but no words come. "Who's gonna farm?" It's a timeless question, one inexorably linked to the arc of our human story. Studying his expression, I discover that he's looking through me, past me, to a point somewhere along the distant edge of the fields. Across the way, an old market truck fires to life, six cylinders knocking an insistent rhythm. Joseph's eyes find mine again.

"I hope the farm will still be around for my grandson," the old farmer says at last. "I plan to be here. What else can I do? I'll do my best."

STRABERRY SHRUB

From Heritage Hollow Farms

Inspired by Joseph Fields Farm

Makes about 2½ cups (20 ounces)

A refreshing soda substitute, this is also a fun project for kids to help make! Serve chilled with mineral water (about 1 part shrub to 4 parts water; modify to taste) or enjoy drizzled over yogurt or ice cream.

1 quart ripe strawberries, washed, trimmed, and quartered

1 cup sugar or local honey, or to taste

1 cup apple cider vinegar*

1. Mash the berries in a medium bowl and cover with sugar. Let sit until a syrup forms—depending on the ripeness of the berries, this could be several hours or overnight.

2. Purée the berries using an immersion blender. Strain the puréed berries through a fine-mesh strainer placed over a bowl, pressing them with the back of a spoon to release more pulp; you should have very little pulp, if any, in the strainer to discard. Whisk in the apple cider vinegar.

3. Transfer to a jar, seal, and refrigerate to chill.

*Bragg's Organic Apple Cider Vinegar tastes great with this.

WATERMELON JUICE

From Heritage Hollow Farms

Inspired by Joseph Fields Farm

Serving size varies, depending on the size of the melon

1 small watermelon

Watermelon juice is incredibly hydrating and invigorating, especially on hot days out in the field.

Quarter the watermelon and remove the flesh from the rind.* Place the watermelon flesh in a blender or food processor and process until smooth. Pour the juice into a container (in general, you'll need a 1-quart jar for a small melon). Chill and enjoy (this doesn't keep long so drink after chilling).

*Freeze the rind pieces for your dog to eat on a hot day. Dogs love watermelon, too!

BOILED PEANUTS

From Heritage Hollow Farms

Inspired by Joseph Fields Farm

Makes 1 pound boiled peanuts

1 pound raw peanuts
(unroasted, in-shell)
¼ cup salt + extra as needed
4 cups water

1. Rinse the peanuts to remove any dirt.

2. Place the peanuts and salt in a large stockpot and add the water. Bring to a boil, cover, and continue to boil for about 3 hours.

3. Taste the peanuts; if you want softer peanuts, it will require extra time. Season with additional salt, if desired.

17

GARCIA ORGANIC FARMS

FALLBROOK, CALIFORNIA

Organic citrus and other tree fruits

O n a mountaintop in Southern California, Juan Garcia slices a wedge of plump grapefruit. "Taste this," he says, equal parts command and suggestion, and I take the offering obediently. The grapefruit is unlike any I've ever tasted, floral and buttery, only a passing note of bitterness to balance the sweet. Known as Oro Blanco, it's hardly reminiscent of the pucker-inducing citrus sold at my local East Coast grocery store. Juan studies my reaction before smiling.

"People think we can't grow fruit like this," he says, gesturing toward crates of tangerines, lemons, and oranges bound for local farmers' markets. "Citrus with this flavor, this quality. But we do, and organically, too. We're showing everyone that this can be done."

Equidistant between Los Angeles and San Diego, Juan's farm spills down two sides of a rough mountain slope. The thickly planted hillsides are flush with avocados, figs, and more than two dozen varieties of citrus. "When I bought my first nine acres, in 1988, there was nothing here," he recalls. "Just rocky bare land. Over the years, we bought a second parcel, then a third. Today we have almost thirty acres in full production."

These days, Garcia Organic Farms would fit most people's definition of paradise. The air is perfumed with orange blossoms, and warm breezes

carry a bouquet of ripening fruit. Honeybees bounce from flower to flower beneath trees brimming with birdsong. As we climb the steep slopes of the mountainside, Juan recalls just how far he's come.

"I moved here from Mexico when I was seventeen, in 1975. I was tiny, a hundred and twenty pounds. No one wanted to hire me! When I finally got a job, I only made a dollar an hour.

"Eventually," he continues, "I found a mentor. An old farmer took me under his wing, taught me how to grow citrus. How to farm this rocky land. He passed away just last year, at the age of ninety-three. I'm very grateful to him."

The day is bright and warm, and a soft spring sun filters through the leaves of the citrus groves. Suddenly, from the shadows, a floppy-eared German shepherd bounds toward us.

"*Hola*, Comanche," the farmer says happily, greeting the dog. "Don't worry, he doesn't bite. In fact," he adds, laughing, "he doesn't even bother to bark."

The trees are laden with citrus, from thumb-size kumquats to fist-size Valencias, bright yellows and oranges suspended among the waxy green leaves. Juan pauses to pick a lime called a Palestine Sweet, slicing it lengthwise and passing me half. I've barely enjoyed its honeydew melon flavor before he thrusts a wedged blood orange into my hand, immediately followed by a sunny slice of lemon. It's as though I'm walking through a life-size fruit salad.

Accustomed to the strict seasonality of my Shenandoah Valley farm, I often forget that citrus is a winter fruit, at its peak when most farms are snow-covered and dormant. "Yes," Juan nods, "we have that advantage. But because we make our living solely through farmers' markets, part of the challenge is there's

Juan's Farming Wisdom

"I learned from my mentor that if you grow great food, you don't have to spend a penny on advertising. Word of mouth will take care of it for you."

no citrus to sell in the summer. To stretch the season, we grow eight different kinds of tangerines, and these days we've got them from November all the way through June. The orange trees will produce until about April, and if we have a good season, we can grow grapefruit all winter and into late spring. Summer is for figs, persimmons, and mulberries."

Pausing at what appears to be a nondescript, fruitless bush, Juan beckons excitedly. "We're always trying new varieties, and not many people are growing these yet." He pushes aside the leaves, revealing a dozen slim, green pods similar to okra in shape and size. Plucking one, the farmer cuts it in half.

"These are called Finger Limes, and they're a new variety for us. But that's not the fun part—when you squeeze them, they look just like caviar. See?" He applies a slight pressure, and the fruit bursts from the pod, shimmering like pink roe. Beneath the bright sunlight, a hundred spheres of citrus glisten between his fingertips. "Beautiful, huh? Chefs use these on salads, to add a little color. It's just a fun thing we do to keep things interesting."

Like most sustainable farms I've visited, Juan's operation has remarkably little infrastructure. His main building is a small warehouse that serves triple duty: packing shed, workshop, and market truck garage. As we enter the shaded building we pause near crates of fresh citrus packed for delivery to Santa Monica.

"We pick the fruit the day before we send it to market so it's as fresh as it can be. That way, there's no need for storage. As for equipment, I have a small loader to help with planting and for pushing out old trees. That's pretty much all there is to it. Other than that, labor is my biggest expense."

The farm's soil is a gritty, sandy clay, and on the steep slopes, scattered pebbles make the footing especially treacherous. It's nearly impossible to retain moisture in soil like this, and with annual rainfall comprising less than twenty inches, it makes the task all the more daunting. However, while the neighboring hills appear withered and barren, Juan's farm is covered in a lush understory of greenery. Knee-high grains, legumes, and wild grasses spread a living blanket across the feet of his fruit trees.

"It might look a little weedy," he explains, "but a cover crop like this is incredibly important." He kneels beside a pomelo tree, where wild mustard, oats, and alfalfa nod drowsily in

Juan's Farming Wisdom

"There's no such thing as a perfect season. One year we get seventy-five thousand pounds of avocados, the next year a freeze wipes us out. We learn to take life as it goes."

the warm spring breeze. "These plants help protect the roots, preventing erosion and keeping the soil temperatures cool. Once a year, I get my guys to weed-whack it all, turning it into mulch. The next year, it grows back on its own."

This cycle of sustainability is a common thread running through the farm. I ask him if he'd ever want to expand production, purchasing more land from the rocky, fallow fields that surround his property.

"No," he replies definitively, "I'm happy with what I've got. Getting bigger doesn't mean getting better. Agriculture is unpredictable to start with, and when one little thing goes wrong, the enterprise can quickly fall apart. My hands are full. Besides," he adds with a smile, "I have eight grandchildren now, and I want to spend time with them."

Halfway up a dusty trail, an aged Toyota pickup truck that's missing its doors is being loaded with oranges. Farmhands Jesus and Rudolpho seem calibrated to the steep, pebbly grade, leaning backward as they pick their way down the hill. Comanche flops into the shade beneath the truck as the men unload their harvest bags, each encumbered with fifty pounds of fruit.

"This is what most people don't understand about organic farming," Juan says. Rudolpho gently unfurls the canvas of his bag, and the oranges yield a bass rumble as they roll into the crate. "Labor is the number one cost on a farm like ours. Instead of taking shortcuts with chemicals and machinery, we use our hands—and our backs—to get the job done. Naturally, the farmer has to pay his people well, and I believe we do that here. But it certainly comes with a higher cost.

"That's why I like farmers' markets," he continues, "because people understand this. The customers realize they're getting higher quality, and they'll pay a little more for it. Every once in a while, I'll have a big restaurant or grocery store call me up, saying, 'Hey, we want to buy everything you've got.' But you know what? I refuse them every time. I tell them I'm going to take care of the customers I've already got, the families who've supported us at the market over the years."

Letecia's Health Tip

"Sweet limes have twice as much vitamin C as any other citrus, so at the first sign of a cold I juice two limes and mix them with honey. It's been our family remedy for years."

He leans over the tailgate, inspecting the harvest, sorting a few oranges into different crates. "The people at farmers' markets are like a friendship," he continues, "like a family. Sometimes I tell customers, 'Oh, you can take that, have a little extra.' 'No,' they tell me, and would you believe they won't take it? They want to pay me, because they know what we're going through. Once you build your relationships, it really changes how the business works."

We pass a copse of squat trees, bejeweled with what appears to be oversize yellow oranges.

"Why do these oranges look like lemons?" I ask.

"Because they *are* lemons," Juan laughs. "What, you've never seen a lemon the size of a softball?" He shakes his head. "No, you'll rarely see these in the stores. The skin is too delicate.

These are Meyer Improved, and they don't transport well. We take them to market, but of course they must be handled very gently. Go ahead, feel how different the skin is."

The distinction is evident at first touch. The lemons I'm accustomed to have a thick, almost rubbery peel, but this fruit has a skin reminiscent of fine suede. I can't imagine them netted into bags, tossed onto trucks, and heaped along the produce aisle. Juan acknowledges this, explaining that most fruit that we find in stores is selected for its ability to be shipped long distances. The farmer stops in the middle of the road, adjusts his cowboy hat, and faces me.

"Look. You gotta love this life, this business. You'd be crazy to go through this trouble if you didn't believe in what you're doing." He gestures toward the tree. "Who wants to put this much work into getting a lemon to market? No, I figured out a long time ago it couldn't be just about the money. It's a beautiful way to live, this kind of farming."

His sons Armando, thirty-five, and Joel, twenty-nine, agree. "I never appreciated it until I moved away," Armando tells me later that afternoon. "When you're a kid, growing up on the farm all you see is work. Then you move to the city, but it's too fast-paced, too crazy. You're either going a hundred miles

Armando's Farm Humor

"Sometimes it's tempting, but at farmers' markets, vendors should never date other vendors. Markets are like a big family, and people will gossip for a whole year! Not worth the hassle."

an hour, or you're stuck in traffic. Now that I've got perspective, I love it here."

Juan's sons travel to farmers' markets each week to sell the family produce. "When we first started doing markets in 1990," Armando recalls, "it was so much harder. We were one of the few organic citrus farms back then, and people just weren't ready for it. It's gratifying to have stuck around, to see things catching on. The past ten years, the customer support has just been incredible."

It was a scene I had already witnessed firsthand. Early Saturday morning in downtown Santa Monica, Juan's stall was a sunny spotlight in the center of market, his tables laden with a color-wheel of yellows, greens, and oranges. Customers gathered fresh fruit by the bagful, grapefruit and tangerines as bright as baubles. With daughter Sophia cradled on one hip, Armando cheerfully greeted shoppers, answering questions and making quick change, steadily restocking the array of fruits they had brought from the rugged mountains of Temecula.

Back at the farm, Juan Garcia's grandchildren come rushing out of the house. He sweeps young Sophia into his arms, and she giggles and squirms as her grandfather makes faces, cooing in baby Spanish. He gently lowers her, and she runs to her mother, Letecia.

"Can there be more farms like this?" Juan asks, repeating my question. "Yes. I can see the potential. But we've got to have more young people in the business. The economics are

Juan's Farm Humor

"My family gets so mad when I come to market, because I want to give everyone a discount. My sons say, 'Dad, I know you own this business, but don't burn us!' As a farmer, of course you have to make a profit, but you want to share, too."

certainly there. I keep asking, though: Where's the next generation?"

He pauses, watching his grandchildren chase one another across the lawn, playing in the cool shade of palm and macadamia trees. "Our schools teach us if we go to college, the bigger the degree, the bigger the money." Juan pushes back his cowboy hat.

"You know what I say to that? *Baloney.* It's how hard you want to work," the farmer says, making a fist to punctuate his point. "That's what makes a person successful."

BLOOD ORANGE MARMALADE

From Heritage Hollow Farms

Inspired by Garcia Organic Farms

Makes about 1 to 2 pints (typically fills two to four ½-pint canning jars)

Sweet and slightly tangy, this is the perfect accompaniment for the Anytime Biscuits on page 134. For more information on canning, see page 295.

1 pound (about 4 to 5 medium) blood oranges
About 3 cups water
1½ cups sugar, or to taste

1. Wash the oranges, then slice off both ends of each one. Cut the oranges in half and remove any seeds and extra pith. Leave the rinds on.

2. Using a sharp paring knife, thinly slice the oranges, then cut each slice in half, continuing to slice them until you reach your preferred segment size for the marmalade (some people like their orange slices to be smaller triangles, while other prefer larger half-moons).

3. Place the orange pieces in a bowl and add enough water to fully submerge the fruit. Cover the bowl and let it sit overnight to soften the rinds.

4. The next day, pour the entire mixture into a medium saucepan and bring it to a boil. Reduce the heat and simmer for about 30 minutes, until the rinds are softened.

5. Whisk in the sugar, mixing until it's fully dissolved. Increase the heat and boil for 25 to 30 minutes, stirring frequently. Test the marmalade for doneness by dropping some onto a chilled plate—if it wrinkles, it's ready. It should not be watery, and will have some density to it.

6. Place the marmalade in sterilized canning jars, seal, and process in a hot water bath for 10 minutes before storing.

GUACAMOLE

From Garcia Organic Farms

Serves 4 to 6

6 ripe avocados (use whatever variety is in season)

1 tomato, diced

¼ onion, diced

2 jalapeño or serrano chiles, diced

Juice of 1 lemon

Sea salt

Peel and pit the avocados, then place them in a bowl and mash them. Add the tomato, onion, chiles, and lemon juice, and stir to combine.* Season with salt to taste.

*The lemon juice will preserve the guacamole and prevent it from browning as quickly. Another, more peculiar tip: If you place an avocado pit back into the dip, it will also help prevent browning.

CHOCOLATE AVOCADO MOUSSE WITH GRAPEFRUIT

From Heritage Hollow Farms

Inspired by Garcia Organic Farms

Serves 4 to 6

1 large ripe avocado

¼ cup coconut milk or almond milk

¼ cup unsweetened cocoa powder (adding a teaspoon or so more will increase the richness)

2 teaspoons local honey or sugar, or to taste

1 teaspoon vanilla extract

Grapefruit slices

The tangy, citrusy flavor of the grapefruit nicely complements the richness of the chocolate and avocado in this mousse.

1. Peel and pit the avocado. Place the avocado in a blender and process until smooth.

2. Combine the milk, cocoa, sugar, and vanilla in a bowl and stir until fully incorporated. Add the cocoa mixture to the avocado and process until completely incorporated.

3. Refrigerate for at least fifteen minutes, until chilled through. Serve individually or in a large serving bowl, garnished with fresh grapefruit slices.

18

RIVERVIEW FARMS

RANGER, GEORGIA

Grass-finished beef, free-range pigs,
and organic corn and soy

I n northwest Georgia, just outside the hamlet of Ranger, Rango the farm dog is bounding through buttercups. "He's only a year old," Charlotte Swancy says, almost apologetically. Rango sprints across the pasture, bluegrass and timothy bending in his wake, abandoned in thralls of puppy glee. "It's a good place for a farm dog," she continues. "Or a farm kid. Or, you know, just about anyone."

Taking in the view, I understand exactly what she means. For the past three days this southernmost tip of Appalachia has been lashed with rain, but today the clouds have parted just enough for the sun to peek through. Spring has arrived. White clover, snowy heads in full bloom, bob on the slight breeze. Red oak and sweet gum are in leaf, and along the edge of the woods, an enormous boar hog, ears flopped forward over his red mottled face, grunts his approval.

"That's Power Line," says Wes, Charlotte's husband and swine-farmer-in-chief around these parts. "It's been a tough winter, and he's just as happy to be enjoying the warmer temperatures. And don't worry," he adds, seeing me stare at the boar's frothy jowls, "when he gets excited, he foams a little at the mouth. Come springtime, he's got work on his mind."

As if on cue, two large sows emerge from the depths of the forest, sizing up Power Line appraisingly. No shrinking violets, the ladies tip the scales

at five hundred pounds apiece and aren't afraid to flaunt it. Cue the mood music: Riverview is bringing pig booty back. A few oinks and snorts later, all three disappear into the woods, moving with startling speed for their size. Wes leans against a fence post, watching them go. "That's the way it works around here. Nature taking its course."

Nature pushes every edge of Riverview Farms, forests and mountains and sweetly rolling hills. The Coosawattee River forms the northernmost boundary, eleven hundred acres of pasture and fields nestled between Chattanooga and Atlanta, an hour northwest and southeast, respectively. "We grow our own grain here on the farm, all certified organic," Charlotte says. "Wes finishes the hogs on corn, and his twin brother, Brad, mills it to sell to whiskey distilleries. Moonshine," she elaborates. "That's all the rage right now. Of course, he also makes grits." She laughs. "Grits and moonshine, two ends of the spectrum. We try to stay balanced around here."

Along the river, garlic is sprouted knee-high, flourishing in the rich sediments of the flood plain. Rango rips through the thick green tops, paw prints trailing through the moist, dark loam. The rows are planted twenty bulbs across, extending like a landing strip to the distant woods. "We've got a vegetable CSA—

Community Supported Agriculture—about one hundred and fifty subscriptions. The rest of the produce goes to our Farm Mobile, down in Atlanta. This'll be our third year sending out the truck, and it's exceeded all expectations."

The Farm Mobile is a retired linen truck, repurposed and modified to be a farmers' market on wheels. Throughout the week the yellow-and-green box truck can be found parked in "food deserts" in downtown Atlanta, areas of the city with limited access to fresh fruits and vegetables, or in neighborhoods where traditional supermarkets have pulled out. On other days, they collaborate with local businesses to bring veggies to company employees, an unexpected perquisite of a job in the city. "It was just something that needed to be done, so we did it," Charlotte says. "That's how most of our projects get started. Identifying a need."

Brad's grain mill is a perfect example. He currently works with three distilleries, and the phone keeps ringing. I find him grinding grain in a dusty room near the machine shop, silvery kernels of corn tumbling from the hopper.

"Where are you going to find locally grown organic corn, milled fresh like this?" He dips his hands beneath the screen and sifts coarsely ground corn through his fingers. The machine rumbles in a deep baritone. With global demand for bourbon and whiskey at an all-time high, business is certainly poised to boom. Corn mash offers an easily transportable product, positioning a local farm on the cutting edge, potentially, of a worldwide marketplace.

It's no accident that Riverview targets urban sales channels, focusing most of its attention on metro-area Atlanta. "We've got about five folks in our hometown who regularly shop with us," Charlotte laughs. "*Five.*" Her face turns serious. "I mean, don't get me wrong. We're grateful for their support. But that's not going to keep our farm going, so we focus most of our efforts on Atlanta. Besides, at the end of the day, we owe it to those five people, making sure we stay in business for them."

A sinuous road runs along the forest's edge, the red clay scattered with twin rivulets of bright pebbles. Above, the rain-washed sky is decorated with thin stratus clouds, breezy as linen warmed on a clothesline. The day has turned bright and promising, and Charlotte studies the distant hills pensively.

"Wes and I went to college to study chemistry. I planned to go on to med school; Wes wanted to be a professor." She pauses thoughtfully. "All along, we always wanted to teach, to help. But this is where life shifted us, I suppose, helping people improve their health through a good diet."

Her expression becomes clouded. "There was a moment, though, where we weren't so sure about our decision. It was our second year farming, the middle of summer, and we had a beautiful crop of vegetables in the field. Then right before harvest, a huge hailstorm rolled through and wiped everything out. I mean, it was devastating. I turned to Wes and said, 'That's it. I'm out, I can't do it anymore.' Right away, I started looking for a new job.

"So I sent out my résumé, and got an offer from a pharmaceutical company. But just before I was about to work for them, something spoke to me: *This is where you need to be, on the farm.* The next day, I turned down the job. I've been here ever since, and never regretted it."

Amazingly, the farm now provides twelve full-time salaries, an enormous accomplishment. Purchased by Wes's father, Carter, in 1975, it took nearly thirty years before the farm generated enough income to support even one salary, much

"When selling directly to customers, ramping up production can be almost as hard as it is to dial it back. We do our best to grow as the market allows us."

less a dozen. Carter, now sixty-seven, is a stout, weather-beaten farmer with hands that bespeak a lifetime of hard work. Charlotte and I find him with his youngest son, Drew, replacing bearings on a seed planter, preparing for the new season ahead.

"You never wake up on a farm—anybody's farm—where there isn't a flat tire somewhere," Carter jokes, his eyes twinkling with good humor. His tone is worn smooth by years of hard-won wisdom. "That's just something you accept on a farm, learn to live with."

Drew hammers home a new bearing, and the sound of clanking metal rings through the bright Georgia morning. "We're feeding high magnesium salt licks to the cattle right now," Carter continues, "because the rye grass is flush after all this rain." His son flips the bearing, holds it at eye level to examine his work, then gives it a few more taps.

"This time of year," Drew explains, joining the conversation, "they'll get grass tetanus, and can die before you know it." He ducks beneath the planter and reaches for his ratchet. "Always something to stay on top of, right?"

Carter nods his agreement. "It only takes two or three slip-ups, and you're in real trouble in this business. Those cows have to go into the fall with good body condition, or a winter like the one we just had will knock them back." He removes his cap, wiping sweat from his brow. "Last summer, it rained so much the hay didn't hold its nutrients, so we couldn't count on feed to carry us through. Now, it's more rain again, so we've got minerals to worry about, then the summer grass slump, on account of the heat."

He passes Drew a 9/16-inch socket, stooping low beneath the planter. "If we can somehow get ahead," he continues, straightening, "we'll plant Sudan grass, maybe sorghum. But it's hard to do all that unless you're turning a good profit."

The old farmer sits heavily on the step board of the planter, his eyebrows knitted in thought. "We grow our own grain here, right? So take organic versus conventional soybeans for example." He points to the fields near the river bottom, ready for planting. "The organic beans out there right now, we can maybe get forty, forty-five bushels out of them. But the genetically modified beans—the ones made for use with chemicals, you understand—they'll put out seventy-five bushels." Carter stares at me intently, letting his point sink in. "Now listen. We're certified organic, and our yields are slowly improving, but you gotta do the math. Somebody has to pick up the difference. Unless we get a higher price for raising this food naturally, then we won't be in business for long."

I hear him loud and clear. More often than not conventional farming resembles a sine curve, where annual chemical inputs are required to buoy otherwise decreasing yields. Organic farming, however, typically follows a more gradual trajectory, requiring years—even decades—to restore soil health. It's a classic tortoise-versus-hare situation: To compete with farms that rely on herbicides and commercial fertilizers, organic farmers have to commit to a long-ranging visionary plan. Scores of independent researchers have proven this to be true, and for producers like Carter, who take a multigenerational view, the long-term rewards outweigh the allure of a quick payday. But for other farmers, buried in debt and with little ability to directly market their crops, more bushels per acre often seems like the only logical choice.

At a farm like Riverview, a diversified offering of pork, vegetables, and grains certainly helps as well. But it's grass-finished cattle that dominate the landscape these days, and the farm does its best to meet what has been a meteoric rise in demand. The cattle are processed at a local abattoir, and the cuts sold at Atlanta farmers' markets and restaurants each weekend.

"We raise one hundred and sixty, one hundred and seventy head a year," Charlotte says, "all black Angus. About five years

Charlotte on Working with Chefs

"I think texting is the greatest invention when it comes to restaurants. In the past, when we'd call to check an order, the chefs would always be so grouchy on the phone! With texting, you get the information without all the grumpiness."

ago, we took a lease on the University of Georgia's research grass farm. It was perfect timing. Only a few miles from us, and already set up with fences and water. Six hundred acres of perfect pasture," she marvels. "It would have been a crime *not* to farm it."

We drive the short distance to the grass farm, wet asphalt wending through the wooded countryside. A sharp left turn, and the forest opens into an ocean of buttercups, petals bright as sunshine, a *Wizard of Oz* moment as flowers seem to stretch into infinity. Beyond the high tensile fence, Angus cattle dip their heads below the golden canopy, munching spring garlic and wild oats, a succulent vernal salad. Their winter coats are thickly curled and just beginning to turn from brown to black, a reminder of the brutal winter that was. With February snows long gone, the cattle will soon be doffing their overcoats. Today, frogs are singing, honeybees are buzzing, and the entire farm seems ready for spring.

First popularized in the American mainstream by Michael Pollan's *The Omnivore's Dilemma*, grass-finishing cattle on pasture is an ancient agricultural practice, a simple recipe of photosynthesis, rainfall, and patience. Though they require a few more months to mature than their grain-finished brethren—typically twenty-four months versus eighteen—when properly raised, grass-finished cattle produce remarkably flavorful and tender beef. Most important, by finishing solely on grass and never supplementing grain, emphasis is focused entirely on sustainability: carbon sequestration, moisture retention, and biological diversity. Under conscientious management, grass-based systems offer a compellingly sustainable option over corn-fed beef, famously documented for its heavy reliance on fossil fuels, water, and antibiotics.

Still, just as Carter pointed out, environmentalism and economics must remain correlatives, and longer finishing time, coupled with trucking, processing, and marketing costs, creates its own unique challenges. The farmers believe their sustainable vision will pay off in the long run. Faith, however, remains a finicky metric to quantify.

We pick our way along a rain-soaked road, traversing an obstacle course of mud puddles. The cattle study us as we pass, pausing mid-bite with orchard grass hanging from the corners of their mouths. It's been a full day, complete with prancing pigs, crunching corn, and puppies galloping through garlic. Now, a field of cows and spring buttercups almost overwhelms the senses.

"All combined, we estimate our farm feeds fifteen hundred people a week," Charlotte volunteers. "That's pretty good for a little farm in Georgia, don't you think? And we believe we can do even better."

She regards the cattle, grazing contentedly in the dappled shade of the pin oaks. "One farm isn't going to feed the world. We know that. But a bunch of family farms, working together toward that goal?" A warm Georgia breeze moves through the wild flowers, and she smiles. "I like to think it's possible."

Did You Know?

While nearly all cattle in the United States are born onto pasture, only a small percentage are allowed to remain there. At around six months of age, the overwhelming majority of steers and heifers are sent to feedlots to finish on corn and other grains. In contrast, demand for grass-finished meats has grown by double-digits annually since the late 1990s.

HERBED BUTTER POPCORN

From Heritage Hollow Farms

Inspired by Nichols Farm & Orchard and Riverview Farms

Makes about 8 cups popcorn

1. Mix together the butter and the herbs, then add a sprinkle of sea salt. Heat over low heat until melted. Set aside.

2. Heat a large saucepan over medium heat and add the coconut oil. When the oil is melted, add the popcorn kernels. Cover the pot and cook the popcorn, shaking the pot occasionally as the kernels pop.

3. Watch closely and remove the pot from the heat as soon as the popping slows; this should take less than 4 minutes. Shake the pot once more to double-check that the kernels have finished popping.

4. Open the lid, drizzle the popcorn with the herbed butter, and toss to mix.

2 tablespoons unsalted butter, room temperature

Finely chopped fresh or dried thyme and rosemary

Sea salt

3 tablespoons coconut oil

1/3 cup popcorn kernels

THE PERFECT GRILLED GRASS-FED RIB-EYE STEAK WITH CHIMICHURRI

From Heritage Hollow Farms

Inspired by Riverview Farms

Serves 1

One 1-pound grass-fed
bone-in rib-eye steak

Celtic sea salt

Freshly cracked black pepper

1 tablespoon grass-fed butter

Chimichurri (recipe follows)

ote that the chimichurri must be made at least 12 hours before you plan to serve the steak.

1. Allow the steak to reach room temperature before cooking. (It will cook more evenly if it is not cold.)

2. Preheat the grill to the highest setting. Season both sides of the steak liberally with salt and pepper.

3. Place the steak on the grill and cook for 2 minutes, then rotate the steak roughly 60 degrees and cook for another 2 minutes. Turn the steak over and repeat this process with the other side.*

4. Remove the steak from the grill and place a pat of butter on top. Let the steak rest for 4 minutes.

5. Serve the steak with chimichurri on the side.

*Don't mess with the steak more than you have to—excessive movement of the steak on the grill will lead to uneven cooking. Always make sure to use tongs when handling your steak; no forks or knives. And trust the cooking times! An 8-minute cooking time will cook a 1-pound, grass-fed rib eye to rare-medium-rare. Grass-fed steaks are best enjoyed at this temperature.

CHIMICHURRI

1 cup water

1 tablespoon Celtic sea salt

2 cups olive oil

1 cup red wine vinegar

2 cups chopped fresh flat-leaf parsley

1 cup chopped fresh oregano

1 garlic head, cloves peeled and minced

1 teaspoon red pepper flakes

1. Combine the water and salt in a small saucepan and bring to a boil. Set aside.

2. Combine the oil, vinegar, parsley, oregano, garlic, and pepper flakes in a 1-quart mason jar. Add the warm salt water and tightly close the lid. Shake to combine. Refrigerate for at least 12 hours before using.

BRAISED BEEF SCALOPPINE

From Conne Ward-Cameron at Riverview Farms

Inspired by Riverview Farms

Serves 2 to 4

6 tablespoons unsalted butter

2 tablespoons olive oil

½ cup unbleached all-purpose flour

½ teaspoon salt

½ teaspoon freshly ground pepper

1½ pounds grass-fed chuck steak, trimmed, thinly sliced, and pounded to ⅛-inch thickness

½ cup white wine

1 cup beef stock

Cooked pasta for serving

FARMER'S NOTE: *Atlanta-area chefs tell us they enjoy working with grass-fed beef because they appreciate the taste, saying it's a piece of meat that tastes like meat. "There's a whole lot to the process of taking care of the cows, from how they're grown to how they're butchered. With grass-fed beef I feel that the quality is there from start to finish. They want to produce something that tastes really good," says Lynne Sawicki of Sawicki's Meat, Seafood and More in Decatur, Georgia. Braising is an especially great way to cook a cut of grass-fed beef taken from the animal's working muscle group, since going low and slow with a little liquid helps keep the meat tender.*

1. Melt 2 tablespoons of the butter with the oil in a large skillet over medium-high heat.

2. Combine the flour, ½ teaspoon salt, and ½ teaspoon pepper in a large shallow dish (such as a pie plate).

3. Dip each slice of beef in the flour mixture to coat both sides. Shake off any excess flour.

4. Place a few slices of beef in the hot butter and oil mixture. Do not crowd the pan. Brown each slice quickly, cooking for about 1 minute per side, and transfer to a plate. Cover the cooked slices to keep them warm while you repeat with the remaining beef, adding addition butter as needed.

5. Pour the fat from the skillet. Add the wine, bring to a boil, scraping up any browned bits in the pan, and cook until reduced, about 2 minutes. Reduce the heat to a simmer, then add the stock and return the beef slices to the pan. Cover the pan and cook for 15 minutes, or until the beef is tender. Uncover and continue simmering until the sauce thickens, about 5 minutes. Season with salt and pepper. Mix the cooked pasta in with the sauce until warmed through; serve.

EPILOGUE

In February, many months after my farm visits, I was cutting wood when the sky suddenly darkened. A fierce squall unleashed sideways snow, quickly driving me inside the house. I shrugged out of my work coat, embracing the warmth of my kitchen, and clicked on the radio. An arctic blast, the meteorologist said, stretched nationwide: Cape Cod was buried waist-deep in snow, upper Minnesota was locked in negative digits, and even Dallas barely hovered above freezing. Frigid winds gusted all the way to Charleston, South Carolina, where Joseph Fields' banana tree, I imagined, must have been shaking in its roots. I placed a kettle on the stove, warming my ashen hands beside the burner, and wondered how my fellow farmers were coping with the harsh conditions.

A short while later, I sat near the window cupping my hot mug of tea as the wind howled outside, bending the leafless boughs of sycamores and black walnuts. I reminisced back to warmer days, to sunny citrus on a California mountaintop, and birdsong drifting from Iowan shade trees, to the joy in wading through a sparkling Missouri river. I turned off the radio, watching as the trees bowed and swayed, my thoughts wandering. Eighteen producers; each so unique, yet somehow united. My mind drifted further, recalling a last-second detour, which, over the passing months, had taken on a deeper meaning.

After leaving Joseph Fields Farm I stopped to visit the Angel Oak, a colossal tree many hundreds of years old. Six adults, their arms spread wide and fingertips touching, can barely girdle its circumference, and the branches snake like lightning, each limb a kinetic, spiraling crescendo. Over the centuries this oak has weathered hurricanes, fire, floods, and drought, even a civil war raging around it. Tested beyond all measure, it has responded by rooting itself ever deeper, flourishing against the very elements that might destroy it.

Road signs led me to its parking lot, packed with SUVs and minivans, Priuses and pickups. The license plates represented all corners of the country, and competing political bumper stickers blended into a patriotic blur. Surrounded by fellow sojourners beneath the oak, looking upward we stared wordlessly into the cathedral-like spaces, spellbound. All around conversations fell silent in reverence.

Tens of thousands visit this tree each year, numbers traditionally reserved for sporting events or theme parks or rock concerts. But there were no cheerleaders at the end of this path, no celebrity spokesmice, nor leather-chapped rockers. There was nothing to sell, and nothing to spend. At the end of the well-worn footpath, there was only a solitary, enormous tree.

Months after this experience, I found myself asking questions. Why did people keep coming? What did they hope to discover, to learn? After all, almost everyone has seen a big tree before. We've picnicked beneath their shade, and swung from their sturdy limbs. As children, we climbed every maple in the neighborhood, and as adults, we've daydreamed of poplar-lined Parisian boulevards, or secluded palms on tropical beaches. Dream nearly any dream, and you're sure to find a tree somewhere in the background.

But in the end, these are only dreams. Faced with daily realities, we default to common sense and conventional wisdom, quickly embracing how the real world operates. Undoubtedly, the Angel Oak is a beautiful tree, surely worth ten minutes of our time. But pulling out of the parking lot, we merge onto the highway, locking the accelerator onto cruise control. We check our texts and emails, and update our schedules. And with another scenic diversion behind us, our minds already drifting to new destinations, we quickly fall back into our old habits, repeating the words we've been trained since childhood to ask: *What's in it for me?*

We hear this question—and its affiliates—every day: *Why should I care? Who has the time?* Our world is shaped by these interrogatives, driven by the incessant, disquieting mantras of modern times. Even the hallowed ground of the Angel Oak is no exception. Unspoken beneath the tranquil shade of its boughs, this question remains in the back of our minds, nagging and needling and relentlessly urgent.

What's in it for me?

Confronted with an eternity of problems, this ancient tree knows only solutions. Like a living abacus, it receives our query, processes it, and suggests an answer:

You keep asking the wrong question.

In the presence of such extraordinary beauty, startled into remembering that there are things so much larger than ourselves, we automatically reprioritize and recalibrate, defaulting to language we've somehow forgotten. And this, I believe, is precisely what sustainable farming is all about: the willingness to be inspired, a faith in something greater, and the wisdom to ask a more useful question: What's in it for us?

Change a single word, and change our entire perspective. In 1949, in the wake of World War II, sustainable farmer Aldo Leopold elaborated on this concept in his watershed memoir *A Sand County Almanac*, succinctly bridging the gaps between ecology, philosophy, and economics: "Cease being intimidated by the argument that a right action is impossible because it does not yield maximum profits, or that a wrong action is to be condoned because it pays."

Written more than a half century ago, Leopold's words remain especially relevant, and uniquely suited for the dialogue surrounding our food system. After all, in a culture that values money, prestige, and celebrity above all else, why would anyone choose to look *outward*, embracing a lifestyle that runs fundamentally contrary to the mainstream?

For farmers, there's no guaranteed paycheck or 401K, no benefits package or paid vacations. The work doesn't stop for weekends or holidays, much less for floods or droughts, blizzards or hurricanes. Faced with an endless horizon of physical labor, myriad risks, and meager pay, it's a miracle that anyone would ever choose such a job.

And so, when most of the world asks, *"What's in it for me?"* what unites these people behind a different question entirely?

The reasons are to be found in Nick Muto's steady courage, and Hiu Newcomb's resilience; they shine through in Lloyd Nichols' optimism, and Aba Ifeoma's serene determination. They are rooted in Matt Romero's New Mexican heritage, the charismatic contrariness of Brandon and Susan Pollard, and the plainspoken faith of a man like Joseph Fields, who's preserving his farm for his grandchildren.

These are people who have looked skyward, earthward, and outward. In doing so, they guide us to greater, more important questions: *What do we value? How can we participate? What more can we do?* Questions like these must grow our tomorrows.

And so, pushed by the wind, an acorn falls, discovering the earth. Graced with time, it grows into a tree.

What's in it for us?

ACKNOWLEDGMENTS

FORREST PRITCHARD, author:

Molly Peterson, now the world knows what I already knew: You are a shining talent. Thank you for your amazing good humor, your spontaneity, and for working around my crazy farming schedule. Thanks especially for spearheading the recipe component of the book; I absolutely couldn't have done it without you. Gratitude also goes to Molly's husband Mike—an excellent farmer and chef in his own right—who consistently rearranged his own schedule to help make this project possible.

To Matthew Lore and the entire staff at The Experiment, *THANK YOU*. Your optimism, passion, and willingness to take risks are rare qualities among publishers, and the creative talent you've invested speaks for itself. To Sasha Tropp, my editor, I couldn't have asked for a better collaborator. You knew when to let the process take its own course, and when to ask more from your author. This is a true gift for any writer. And gratitude goes to Allie Bochicchio for adding the final flourishes to the manuscript.

Thank you to my outstanding agent Stephany Evans, who helped navigate several unexpected turns on the road to publication, and who believed in this book the entire way. And special thanks goes to Anna Bliss for championing this project from the start.

To our chef John MacPherson, a HUGE thank you for testing and preparing many of the dishes. Your culinary talents speak through these wonderful photographs. And for anyone considering a weekend getaway—or craving a taste of some of these recipes—I highly recommend John's bed and breakfast in Washington, Virginia, Foster Harris House (www.fosterharris.com).

Carol Blymire, you have been such a help to me over the years, and so generous with your advice and support. Thank you.

To the friends and family members upon whose couches we crashed, my thanks: Susan Marquis, Ralph Tsong, Maureen Sarver, Heather Landry, Amy Schipper, Susie Marshall, Jeanne Floberg, Joan Reishman, Kim O'Donnel and Russ Walker.

Thank you to Alan Mitchell for your ever-amazing editorial contributions, and to my proofreaders David Pratt and Ruth Pritchard, adept at finding those pesky, last-second typos.

Daniel Christensen, thank you for your lovely watercolor gracing the inside covers. And when we were unable to take photographs inside Skyline, thanks goes to Barry Staver for sharing his beautiful pictures.

To my staff at Smith Meadows—Robert Albright, Alec Condon, Chris Rhodes and Travis LaFleur—who skillfully managed the farm as I traveled many Mondays through Thursdays: Thank you. And to Travis, who keeps pestering me about a follow-up to *Gaining Ground*, rest assured. The first chapters are already written.

To my family, Linus, Michelle, Betsy, and Nancy, thank you for believing in me, and in this project. And to my nephew Benson, who reliably asked, "So, did you have a good trip?" each time I returned to the farm. Thanks for asking; it truly meant a lot to me.

To the farmers themselves, including Meg Cattel and Arden Nelson in Colorado, you are an inspiration. This book is my gift to you, and I hope you've enjoyed it as much as I did writing it.

Final thanks goes to you, the reader, for valuing the amazing work these producers do, and for understanding what a true impact your shopping decisions can make. As Wendell Berry eloquently stated, "Eating is an agricultural act." Together, by changing our dialogue and asking new questions, we can cultivate a more sustainable planet, for farmers and customers alike.

MOLLY M. PETERSON, photographer:

First I'd like to thank Forrest for choosing me for this project. You have humbled me with your trust in my talents and abilities, and each and every person we encountered on this journey was a gift for my soul. It was an honor to be a part of this beautiful thing that is so much larger than any of us could have ever anticipated.

There were many smiling faces that shared their homes and meals with us: a welcome and comforting home-away-from-home. I am extra lucky that many were family spread across the country: Jackie, Oliver and Vivi, Ann, Bernard and Philip, Heather, Mandi, Amy Schipper, Deb, Caroline, Joe and Katie, Kinley, Nate and Amanda, Marianne and Marty, Nathan, Barb, Monica, and most especially Grandma (for more than I could ever possibly try to put into words). Ted and Harma, you were both lifesavers and you will never fully know just how needed and appreciated you were at that moment in time. John, Diane, and Sandy at Foster Harris House: It was an absolute joy to work with you all for the first round of recipe photographs; I am deeply grateful for your time, creativity, flexibility, talent and your enthusiasm.

This was one of the most creatively and emotionally consuming projects for me to date, and I had an incredibly supportive team behind me who held down the fort, constantly encouraged me, and fed me when I was grumpy: Mom, Jen, and Pam: Thank you. Alice and Alecia: For years of guidance and love. Corwen, Serian, and Afton: Your smiles and hugs are the very best medicine. To both of my parents: thank you for raising me somewhere I could walk barefoot in the dirt, swim with ponies and goats in the pond, snuggle stinky piglets, and ride my bike to pick up farm-fresh eggs.

Mike, your faith in me and love for me provide the strength I need when I feel my weakest and allow me to shine even brighter when I feel my strongest. Through the travel, the recipe support, and the late-night editing, you were right beside me. After all these years I'm so blessed that we're stronger than ever.

I gathered some of my favorite local farmers and artisans to support the recipe section: Cloud Terre Pottery, Flourish Root, Goat Hill Produce, Waterpenny Farm, The Farm at Sunnyside, Roy & Janets' Orchard, Shire Home Furnishings, Harriet's General, Roxy Daisy, elemenTREE, 1840 Farm, Wild Roots Apothecary, and Kat Habib Pottery.

It's likely that not all proper thoughts of gratitude have been covered here, but do know that each word of encouragement along the way—whether from family and friends, plane seatmates, or my own farm's customers and local community—was stored away for when it was needed most. Thank you.

"If you really want to make a friend, go to someone's house and eat with him . . . the people who give you their food give you their heart."
– *Cesar Chavez*

WHERE TO FIND
THE FARMERS

BLACK OAK HOLLER FARM

Address: 6909 Black Oak Road, Fraziers Bottom, West Virginia 25082

Phone: 740-709-6807

D-TOWN FARM

Website: d-townfarm.com

Address: 14027 West Outer Drive (on the northwestern edge of Rouge Park), Detroit, Michigan 48217

Phone: 313-345-3663

Email: info@detroitblackfoodsecurity.org

Various Detroit-area farmers' markets: visit detroitmarkets.org for more information

GARCIA ORGANIC FARMS

Address: 40430 De Luz Murreta Road, Fallbrook, California 92028

Santa Monica, California–area farmers' markets:

Saturdays at Virginia Avenue Park near Pico Avenue (8:00 A.M.–1:00 P.M.)

Wednesdays at the Promenade (8:30 A.M.–1:30 P.M.)

Saturdays at the Promenade (8:30 A.M.–1:00 P.M.)

Sundays at Ocean Park (8:30 A.M.–1 P.M.)

Direct purchase: Contact Joel Garcia at olivesmamma@yahoo.com or 760-622-0634

HAYSTACK MOUNTAIN GOAT DAIRY

Website: haystackgoatcheese.com

Storefront: 1121 Colorado Avenue, Longmont, Colorado 80501

Haystack products can be found in the following locations:

COLORADO

Boulder County farmers' markets (Boulder and Longmont)

Lucky's Market (Boulder and Longmont)

Alfalfa's Market (Boulder and Louisville)

Flagstaff House (Boulder)

Riff's Urban Fare (Boulder)

Barolo Grill (Denver)

Beast and Bottle (Denver)

Gaia Bistro (Denver)

Marczyk's (Denver)

Potager (Denver)

Rioja (Denver)

Spinelli's Market (Denver)

Splendido (Avon)

Murray's Cheese (throughout the state)

King Soopers (throughout the state)

Whole Foods Market (throughout Colorado, and in select cities in other states)

CHICAGO

Standard Market

Marion Street Cheese

NEW YORK CITY

Murray's Cheese

Stinky Brooklyn

Bedford Cheese Shop

OTHER MARKETS

Bloomy Rind Artisan Cheeses (Nashville, Tennessee)

Caputo's Market (Salt Lake City, Utah)

Four Seasons (Jackson Hole, Wyoming)

Henri's Cheese Shop (Austin, Texas)

St. James Cheese Shop (New Orleans, Louisiana)

The Wedge and Wheel (Stillwater, Minnesota)

Zingerman's Creamery (Ann Arbor, Michigan)

HAYTON FARMS BERRIES

Website: haytonfarmsberries.com

Roadside stand: 16498 Fir Island Road, Mount Vernon, Washington 98273

Seattle-area farmers' markets:

Anacortes	Gig Harbor	Poulsbo
Arlington	Issaquah	Puyallup
Auburn	Juanita Beach	Queen Anne
Ballard	Kent	Redmond
Bayview	Kirkland	Renton
Bellevue	Lake City	Sammamish
Black Diamond	Lake Forest Park	Seattle City Hall
Bothell	Lakewood	Sedro Woolley
Bow	Langley	Shelton
Bremerton	Lynwood	Shoreline
Broadway	Madrona	Silverdale
Burien	Magnolia	Snohomish
Carnation	Maple Valley	South Lake Union
Columbia City	Mercer Island	South Whidbey
Concrete	Mount Vernon	Tacoma
Cross Roads	Mukilteo	Tumwater
Des Moines	Nor Point	University District
Duvall	North Bend	Wallingford
Edmonds	Phinney	West Seattle
Everett	Pike Place Market	Willis Tucker
Federal Way	Port Orchard	Woodinville
Fremont	Port Susan	

JOSEPH FIELDS FARM

Address: 3129 River Road, John's Island, Charleston, South Carolina 29455

Phone: 843-559-5349

Charleston, South Carolina–area farmers' markets:

Mondays at Freshfields Village, Kiawah Island (3 P.M.–dark)

Tuesdays at the Mount Pleasant Farmers' Market (3 P.M.–dark)

Wednesdays at the VA Hospital on Bee Street, Charleston (7:00 A.M.–4:00 P.M.)

Thursdays at the North Charleston Farmers' Market, Park Circle (9:30 A.M.–7:00 P.M.)

Fridays at MUSC, Ashley Avenue, Charleston (7:00 A.M.–4:00 P.M.)

Saturdays at Marion Square, Charleston (8:00 A.M.–2:00 P.M.)

KIYOKAWA FAMILY ORCHARDS

Website: kiyokawafamilyorchards.com

Farm stand: 8129 Clear Creek Road, Parkdale, Oregon 97041

Portland-area farmers' markets:

Beaverton

Courthouse Square

Gresham

Hillsboro

Hollywood

Hood River

King

Lake Oswego

Lloyd Center

Milwaukee

Montavilla

Northwest

Oregon City

Pioneer

Portland State University

Woodstock

Portland-area retailers:

Cherry Sprout Produce

Chuck's Produce and Street Market

Food Front Cooperative Grocery (Northwest and Hillsdale locations)

Green Zebra Grocery

P's and Q's Market

Pastaworks

Rossi Farms

Sheridan Fruit Company

Portland-area restaurants:

Ava Gene's

Celilo Restaurant

The Heathman Restaurant and Bar

Imperial

Multnomah Athletic Club

Nora's Table

Park Kitchen

Screen Door

Timberline Lodge

The University Club of Portland

Urban Farmer Restaurant

The Woodsman Tavern

Portland-area bakeries:

Baker and Spice

Roman Candle Baking Co.

St. Honoré Boulangerie (Northwest and Division locations)

Online retail:

Mikuni Wild Harvest (Mountain Rose apples only; mikuniwildharvest.com)

todayPDX (todaypdx.com)

LAGIER RANCHES

Website: lagierranches.com

Address: 16161 South Murphy Road, Escalon, California 95320

Email: info@lagierranches.com

Bay Area farmers' markets:

Saturdays at San Francisco Ferry Plaza Farmers' Market (8:00 A.M.–2:00 P.M.)

Saturdays at Grand Lake Farmers Market, Oakland (8:00 A.M.–2:00 P.M.)

Sundays at Marin Civic Center Market, San Rafael (8:00 A.M.–1:00 P.M.)

Sundays at Temescal Farmers' Market, Oakland (8:00 A.M.–1:00 P.M.)

Bay Area retailers:

Alameda Natural Grocery (Alameda)

Bi-Rite Market (San Francisco)

Farmer Joe's Market (Oakland)

Fatted Calf Charcuterie (Napa)

Rainbow Grocery (San Francisco)

Berkeley Natural Grocery (Berkeley)

El Cerrito Natural Grocery (El Cerrito)

MATT ROMERO FARMS

Location: Dixon, New Mexico

Santa Fe–area farmers' markets (see santafefarmersmarket.com for more information):

Saturdays in Santa Fe year-round

Tuesdays in Santa Fe during the peak season (June through November)

Thursdays in Los Alamos

Santa Fe–area retailer:
La Montanita Co-op (visit lamontanita.coop for more information)

Santa Fe–area restaurants:

315 Restaurant and Bar

Cafe Pasqual's

Coyote Cafe

Il Piatto

La Boca and Taberna

Lodge of the Four Seasons: Terra Restaurant

Osteria d'Assisi

Sage Bakehouse

Tabla de Los Santos

Educational component: Cooking with Kids, which connects farmers, chefs, and kids in a cooking environment (cookingwithkids.org)

NICHOLS FARM & ORCHARD

Website: nicholsfarm.com

Location: Marengo, Illinois

Chicago-area farmers' markets:

Daley Plaza

Division Street

Elis

Elmhurst

Evanston

Federal Plaza

Green City

Hinsdale

Museum of Contemporary Art

Oak Park

Schaumburg

Wicker Park

CSA shares: See website for more information.

Additional merchants: Numerous Chicago-area restaurants and retailers, including Whole Foods

NICK MUTO AND BACKSIDE BAKES

Location: Cape Cod, Massachussetts

Local clambakes: Backside Bakes (backsidebakes.com)

Domestic retail: Contact Nick Muto at mutonic@aol.com or 508-527-9538

OZARK FOREST MUSHROOMS

Website: ozarkforest.com

Address: 4112 West Pine Boulevard, St. Louis, Missouri 63108

St. Louis farmers' markets:

Maplewood Farmers' Market (Schlafly Bottleworks Brewery, 7260 Southwest Avenue)

Tower Grove Farmers' Market (Tower Grove Park)

St. Louis retailers:

City Greens Market

Larder and Cupboard

Local Harvest Grocery

CSA shares: Fair Shares CCSA (fairshares.org)

On-the-farm vacation (including farm tour): Timber Farms, the Sinks (timberfarmsthesinks.com)

PAUL'S GRAINS

Website: paulsgrains.com

Address: 2475-B 349th Street, Laurel, Iowa 50141

Phone: 641-476-3373

Online retail: See website for more information

POTOMAC VEGETABLE FARMS

Website: potomacvegetablefarms.com

Roadside stands:

Route 7 in Fairfax County, 9627 Leesburg Pike, Vienna, Virginia 22182 (July through October, 10:00 A.M.–6:00 P.M.)

Loudoun County, 38369 John Wolford Road, Purcellville, Virginia 20132 (July through October, 10:00 A.M.–6:00 P.M.)

Washington, DC–area farmers' markets:

Saturdays at Arlington Farmers' Market at the courthouse (April through November, 8:00 A.M.–noon)

Saturdays at Falls Church Farmers' Market (April through November, 8:00 A.M.–noon)

Saturdays at Reston Farmers' Market at Lake Anne Village Center (May through October, 8:00 A.M.–noon)

Saturdays at Leesburg Farmers' Market (May through November, 8:00 A.M.–noon)

Sundays at Takoma Park Farmers' Market (April through November, 10:00 A.M.–2:00 P.M.)

Wednesdays at Crossroads Farmers' Market in Takoma Park (May through October, 11:00 A.M.–3:00 P.M.)

CSA shares: See website for more information

RED LAKE NATION FOODS

Website: redlakenationfoods.com

Location: Redby, Minnesota (approximately 6 miles east of Red Lake on Highway #1; please call ahead for directions if visiting)

Phone: 888-225-2108

Online retail: See website for more information

RIVERVIEW FARMS

Website: grassfedcow.com

Address: 954 White Graves Road Northeast, Ranger, Georgia 30734

Phone: 678-910-2831

CSA shares (see website for more information):

Produce CSA (weekly delivery for thirty weeks)

Meat CSA (monthly delivery year-round)

Atlanta-area farmers' markets:

Morningside Farmers' Market (year-round)

Freedom Farmers' Market (March–December)

Grant Park Farmers' Market (April–December)

Peachtree Road Farmers' Market (April–December)

Atlanta Farm Mobile locations:

Wednesdays in Tucker

Fridays at Sprig restaurant in Oak Grove

Saturdays in Brookhaven

Sundays in Grant Park

Restaurants:

5 Seasons Brewing

Arepa Mia

Avalon Catering

Bacchanalia

Empire State South

The Family Dog

The Gardens at Kennesaw Mountain

Muss and Turner's

Rosebud

Timone's

Watershed on Peachtree

Wrecking Ball Brewpub

RONNYBROOK FARM DAIRY

Website: ronnybrook.com

Address: 310 Prospect Hill Road, PO Box 267, Ancramdale, New York 12503

Phone: 518-398-MILK (6455)

Merchants: Numerous farmers' markets within the New York City metro area and retailers throughout New York state and the surrounding areas (see website for a store locator)

TEXAS HONEYBEE GUILD

Website: txbeeguild.org

Location: Dallas, Texas

Dallas-area farmers' markets:

Coppell Farmers' Market

Dallas Farmers' Market

Vickery Meadow Local Market

White Rock Local Market

Retailers:

Central Market (Dallas and Southlake)

Cox Farms Market (Dallas)

Dude, Sweet Chocolate (Dallas)

eatZi's (Dallas and Grapevine)

Green Grocer (Dallas)

Natural Grocers (Dallas and Denton)

Urban Acres (Dallas)

Restaurants:

The Fairmont Dallas Hotel (Dallas)

Garden Cafe (Dallas)

Hibiscus (Dallas)

Clay Pigeon Food and Drink (Fort Worth)

Potager Cafe (Arlington)

CSA shares:

Eden's Garden CSA Farm (edensorganicgardencenter.com)

Delivery service: Artizone Dallas (artizone.com)

Other merchants:

FreshPoint (Dallas)

Gecko Hardware (Dallas)

Trinity Haymarket (Dallas)

Trinity River Audubon Center (Dallas)

Dogwood Canyon Audubon Center (Cedar Hill)

Ron's Organics (Mesquite)

METRIC CONVERSION CHARTS

TEMPERATURES	
165°F	75°C
250°F	120°C
300ºF	150ºC
325°F	165°C
350°F	180°C
375°F	190°C
400°F	200°C
425°F	220ºC

JAR SIZES	
½-pint	240 ml
1-pint	480 ml
1-quart	950 ml

LIQUIDS	
1 tbsp (only when added to at least ¼ cup)	15 ml
¼ cup	60 ml
⅓ cup	80 ml
½ cup	120 ml
⅔ cup	160 ml
¾ cup	180 ml
1 cup	240 ml
1½ cups	360 ml
2 cups *or* 1 pint	480 ml
3 cups *or* 1½ pints	720 ml
4 cups *or* 2 pints	960 ml

PAN SIZES	
9-inch	23 cm
10-inch	25.4 cm
13 by 9-inch	23 by 33 cm
6-quart	5.7 L

LENGTHS	
¼ inch	6 mm
½ inch	1.3 mm
¾ inch	19 mm / 2 cm
1 inch	2.5 cm
4 inches	10 cm
5 inches	13 cm

WEIGHTS	
1 ounce	28 g
4 ounces	113 g
12 ounces	340 g
1 pound	454 g
1½ pounds	680 g
3 pounds	1.4 kg
4 pounds	1.8 kg

SPECIFIC INGREDIENTS	
1 cup flour	120 g
¼ cup old-fashioned oats	20 g
1 cup oat bran	94 g
1 cup cornmeal	132 g
1 cup panko	53 g
½ cup sugar	110 g
¼ cup honey	80 g
¼ cup brown sugar	36 g
¼ cup cocoa powder	26 g
1 cup chocolate chips (all types)	240 g
1 cup chopped nuts (all types)	90 to 120 g
½ cup shredded coconut	50 g
¾ cup fresh raspberries	100 g
1 cup fresh blueberries	150 g
1 quart fresh strawberries	340 g
1 cup chopped rhubarb	100 g
1 cup chopped fresh herbs (all types)	40 to 45 g
½ cup chopped onion	80 g
1 cup diced pepper	150 g
1 cup diced cooked beets	340 g
1 cup cooked wild rice	164 g
½ cup grated Parmesan cheese	50 g
⅔ cup ketchup	140 g
½ cup lard	113 g
1 cup yogurt or mayonnaise	245 g

GUIDE TO BLANCHING AND CANNING

////////////////////////////////

ABOUT BLANCHING

Blanching produce (scalding vegetables or fruit in boiling water or hot steam for a short time) stops enzyme actions that can cause loss of flavor, color, and texture. Blanching cleanses the vegetables' surface of dirt and organisms, brightens their color, and helps slow down the loss of vitamins. It also wilts or softens vegetables, making them easier to store, and is a necessary step for some produce before storing it in the freezer. The Full-Flavored Collard Greens recipe on page 64 calls for blanching to help retain all the benefits the greens offer.

To blanch, fill a large pot or vegetable blancher with water and bring it to a rolling boil. Clean and cut your produce as needed. Place the pieces in a wire basket or in the perforated blancher insert and immerse them in the boiling water. Cover the pot and start counting the blanching time as soon as the water returns to a boil. Remove the produce from the water immediately.

BLANCHING TIMES	
PRODUCE	**BLANCHING TIME** *(in minutes)*
Artichoke – Globe *(hearts)*	7
Asparagus	
Small stalk	2
Medium stalk	3
Large stalk	4
Beans – Snap, Green, or Wax	3
Beans – Lima, Butter, or Pinto	
Small	2
Medium	3
Large	4
Broccoli *(1½-inch florets)*	3
Steamed	5
Brussel Sprouts	
Small	3
Medium	4
Large	5
Cabbage	
(shredded)	1½
Carrots	
Small	5
Diced or sliced	2
Cauliflower *(florets, 1 inch across)*	3
Celery	3
Corn	
Corn-on-the-cob	
Small ears	7
Medium ears	9
Large ears	11
Whole Kernel or Cream-style	
(ears blanched before cutting corn from cob)	4

PRODUCE	BLANCHING TIME *(in minutes)*
BLANCHING TIMES (continued)	
Greens	
Collards	3
All Other	2
Kohlrabi	
Whole	3
Cubes	1
Mushrooms	5
Whole *(steamed)*	3½
Buttons of Quarters *(steamed)*	3½
Slices *(steamed)*	3
Okra	
Small pods	3
Large pods	4
Onions *(until center is heated)*	3–7
Rings	10–15 seconds
Peas	
Black-Eyed	2
Edible Shell	1½–3
Green	1½
Peppers – Bell	
Halves	3
Strips or Rings	2
Potatoes – New	3–5
Squash – Summer	3
Turnips or Parsnips	2
Cubes	2

ABOUT CANNING

Canning extends the shelf life of produce considerably, and is an excellent way to preserve extra fruit and vegetables. The simplest and most common method of canning is to use a water bath. Water bath canning is appropriate for high-acid foods such as fruits, salsas, and pickles. Most vegetables need to be pressure canned. With water bath canning, you fill glass home-canning jars with acidic food, cover the jars with lids, and then boil them in a pot of water until a seal forms. This forces all of the air out and creates a vacuum, thereby stopping the growth of bacteria and preventing spoilage.

Before beginning the canning process, familiarize yourself with the recipe (such as the Pickled Cherries on page 93 or the Blood Orange Marmalade on page 253), which will provide the required canning time. To start, check your home-canning jars, lids, and bands to make sure they're all fully intact to ensure proper sealing, then wash everything thoroughly. Heat the jars in hot, but not boiling, water until needed; this will prevent them from breaking when hot food is added later. The lids and bands can be kept at room temperature to allow for easy handling.

Prepare the water bath by filling a large pot or water bath canner half full of water. The pot must be big enough to fully submerge the jars in water by 1 to 2 inches. Bring the water to a simmer and continue to simmer until the recipe is prepared. Once the contents are ready, remove a jar from the hot water using a jar lifter or tongs and empty the water that's inside the jar. Fill the jar with the prepared food, leaving ¼ to ½ inch of headspace. Remove any air bubbles. Clean the rim of the jar to remove any residue, then place the lid on the jar. Screw on the band as tightly as possible.

Place the jars onto a canning rack and submerge them in the simmering water bath. Place a lid on the pot and bring the water to a full boil. Begin the processing time. When the time is complete, turn off the heat and remove the lid. Allow the jars to stand in the water bath for 5 minutes to adjust to the temperature. After 5 minutes, remove the jars and place them on a towel to cool. Leave the jars undisturbed for 12 to 24 hours. Do not retighten the bands, which could prevent proper sealing. The lids should not pop up and down when pressed if correctly processed.

RECIPE INDEX

ABOUT THE AUTHOR, PHOTOGRAPHER, AND FOREWORD AUTHOR

FORREST PRITCHARD is a full-time organic farmer who holds degrees from the College of William and Mary. His farm, Smith Meadows, was one of the first "grass-finished," free-range endeavors in the country, and has sold at leading farmers' markets in Washington, DC for more than fifteen years. Pritchard is the author of the *New York Times*–bestselling book *Gaining Ground: A Story of Farmers' Markets, Local Food, and Saving the Family Farm*, picked as a top read by the *Washington Post*, *Publishers Weekly*, and NPR's *The Splendid Table*. The primary blogger for the Facebook page "I Support Farmers' Markets," the largest online farmers' market fan page, he is also a popular public speaker, having given addresses at RAND, Texas Organic Farmers Association, and Weston A. Price International, among others. Pritchard lives with his family on Smith Meadows in Berryville, Virginia.

MOLLY MCDONALD PETERSON has been a professional photographer for more than ten years, from the mountains of Aspen to the Virginia Piedmont. As the former director of photography for two regional food publications that celebrate local and sustainable food and farmers, she was a two-time finalist for the American Society of Magazine Editors' annual "Best Cover" award. Molly is known for her food and farm shoots and has contributed to multiple cookbooks, which she finds amusing since she used to think pancakes came from a box. She lives with her husband Mike, a chef-turned-farmer, in Sperryville, Virginia, where they raise pasture-based livestock on nearly 600 acres of leased land at Heritage Hollow Farms.

DEBORAH MADISON, founding chef of Greens restaurant and writer, is the author of fourteen cookbooks and countless articles on food, cooking, and farming. Her cookbook *Vegetable Literacy* (2013) is the winner of both James Beard and IACP awards. Her latest book is *The New Vegetarian Cooking for Everyone*. She writes for *Zester Daily*, *Lucky Peach*, and Rodale's *Organic Life*.

1. Potomac Vegetable Farms, Vienna, VA

2. Nichols Farm & Orchard, Marengo, IL

3. Hayton Farms Berries, Mount Vernon, WA

4. D-Town Farm, Detroit, MI

5. Ozark Forest Mushrooms, Salem, MO

6. Lagier Ranches, Escalon, CA

7. Haystack Mountain Goat Dairy, Longmont, CO

8. Matt Romero Farms, Dixon, NM

9. Black Oak Holler Farm, Fraziers Bottom, WV

10. Nick Muto and Backside Bakes, Chatham, MA

11. Texas Honeybee Guild, Dallas, TX